The Complete Guide to

Cockatiel Care and Ownership

Lesa Boutin &
Sheila S. Blanchette, CPBC

LP Media Inc. Publishing
Text copyright © 2024 by LP Media Inc.
All rights reserved.

No part of this book may be reproduced or transmitted in any form or by any means, electronic or mechanical, including photocopying, recording, or by an information storage and retrieval system – except by a reviewer who may quote brief passages in a review to be printed in a magazine or newspaper – without permission in writing from the publisher. For information address LP Media Inc. Publishing, 1405 Kingsview Ln N, Plymouth, MN 55447
www.lpmedia.org

Publication Data
Lesa Boutin & Sheila S. Blanchette, CPBC
The Complete Guide to Cockatiel Care and Ownership – First edition.
Summary: "Successfully caring for and owning a Cockatiel"
Provided by publisher.
ISBN: 978-1-954288-85-0
[1. The Complete Guide to Cockatiel Care and Ownership – Non-Fiction] I. Title.

This book has been written with the published intent to provide accurate and authoritative information in regard to the subject matter included. While every reasonable precaution has been taken in preparation of this book the author and publisher expressly disclaim responsibility for any errors, omissions, or adverse effects arising from the use or application of the information contained inside. The techniques and suggestions are to be used at the reader's discretion and are not to be considered a substitute for professional veterinary care. If you suspect a medical problem with your Cockatiel, consult your veterinarian.

Design by Sorin Rădulescu
First paperback edition, 2024

Acknowledgements

Dear Reader,

When our family brought home our first cockatiel many years ago, we had no idea just how enriching and delightful having these curious little parrots as companions would be. Cockatiels, because we've had more than one, stole our hearts with their gentle personalities, amusing antics, and ability to form deep bonds with their human families. However, we also learned that proper cockatiel care requires significant research and commitment.

I wrote this book to share the joys of owning a cockatiel and to provide you with some idea of the responsibilities of caring for these special birds. Too often, cockatiels are purchased on impulse without knowing their specific needs and long life spans. My hope is that this book will allow prospective owners to make an informed decision about bringing a cockatiel into their home.

Lesa Boutin

Sheila S. Blanchette's Acknowledgments

My very heartful thank-you to Lesa Boutin for authoring this book. I am grateful for the opportunity to write a dedicated training chapter on how to build a wonderful companion bird trust through respectful training interaction.

A special thanks to the folks at LP Media and David Anderson for their meticulous work to connect the illustrations to the training words.

I am grateful to my professional animal trainer mentors, whose guidance and insights assisted my decision to become a professional certified parrot behavior consultant (IAABC CPBC). Additionally, I am grateful to the wonderful network of companion bird trainers, thank you for sharing your support.

A special thank you to the animal and avian rescues that have supported my experience with resources and opportunities. Your commitment to advancing companion bird education is commendable, and I am honored to be associated with such esteemed partners. I am deeply grateful to Corrie Butler, Manager/Owner of Rhode Island Parrot Rescue for her friendship, trust, opportunities, and her feedback which all have been invaluable.

I would like to express my deepest gratitude to my loving parents for their unwavering support, and encouragement throughout this journey. I am endlessly grateful for your constant presence in my life. To my husband, Jim, you have been by my side every step of the way. Thank you for believing in me and this project. I love you.

Of Course, to Hei Hei, my adopted cockatiel with allergies to specific bird food and neurological wing issues. Several the steps in the training chapter came from this little cockatiel teaching me about observation and adjusting the environment for improved outcomes. Over the 5 years, he was a wonderful teacher. Sadly, he passed away before this book was published. The Training Chapter is dedicated to him.

To the Readers, if you have read to this point, you are incredible. As you read this book, both authors are trying to bring the latest information to you for having a cockatiel. Paper books can get dated, I tried to keep the training chapter to the latest reference material at the time. The real goal in training is to move away from the force methodology and move toward building trust and choice for the cockatiel methodology. If you need more information on this methodology, please reach out or to a professional certified parrot behavior consultant/trainer. This is a real profession, and there is a need for more parrot behavior trainers/educators so if it you dream it, then follow that dream. Thanks for reading all of this!

"You have a heart of gold for adding a cockatiel into your family. You have a heart of feathers for learning to create a loving, trusting and giving choice relationship with your cockatiel."

Sheila Sullivan Blanchette, CPBC, UW-AAB
Heart of Feathers Education &
Behavior Training for companion birds

TABLE OF CONTENTS

Acknowledgements iii
Sheila S. Blanchette's Acknowledgments iii

CHAPTER 1
Why Choose a Cockatiel? 1
Introduction 1
Basic Traits 3
Basic Anatomy 5
Color Varieties 7

CHAPTER 2
The History of Cockatiels 9
History 9
In the Wild 11

CHAPTER 3
Where to Get Your Cockatiel 15
Chain Pet Stores 16
Exotic Bird and Pet Stores 17
Commercial Breeders 19
Bird Shows 21
Adopting from Local Shelters and Rescues 23

CHAPTER 4
How to Choose Your Cockatiel 25
Choose Wisely 25
Hand-fed Birds 26
Signs and Clues to Look For in a Store or Breeder 27
Individual Bird 30
Should You Get a Male or Female Cockatiel? 32
One Bird or Two? 33

CHAPTER 5
Creating a Home 39
Welcoming Your Cockatiel Home 39
The Right Cage 42
Round Cages 44
New or Used? 45
Cage Placement 46
Cage Bedding 48
Paper Lining 48
Bedding 49
Food and Water Bowls 50
Bath Time 50
Perches 51
Toys, Toys, and More Toys 52
Warnings 54

CHAPTER 6
Dietary Needs 55
Pellets and Seeds 55
Balance 55
Recommended Brands 57
Fruits, Veggies, and Greens 58
Cuttlebone 61
Stubborn Eaters 61
Chop 64
Treats 65
Water 66

CHAPTER 7
Basic Care 67
Cleaning the Cage 68
Grooming 71
Baths 72
Covering the Cage at Night 74
Trimming Flight Feathers 74

CHAPTER 8
Health and Illness 77
Proper Planning 77
Be Vigilant 78
Signs of a Healthy Cockatiel 79
Red Flags 81
Common Cockatiel Health Issues 82

CHAPTER 9
Emotional Health 87
How to Bond with Your Cockatiel 87
Cockatiel Behavioral Issues 89
How Your Body Language Can Affect Your Cockatiel..........93
How to Mentally Stimulate Your Cockatiel 93
DIY..95
Traveling..96
How to Show Your Affection...96
How a Cockatiel Shows Its Affection.......................................97
Interpreting Sounds...98

CHAPTER 10
Training Essentials..99
Why Is Training Important? 99
Understanding the Training Methodology 100
The Basics 102
Target Training 104
Station Training.. 117
Stepping Up Training... 133
Conclusion 149
Additional Resources.. 150

CHAPTER 11

Breeding 151
Be Responsible 151
Unfertilized 152
Bonded Pair 152
Mating Conditions 153
Mating 153
Nesting Box 154
Eggs 155
Signs of Egg Binding 155
Incubation 156
Hatching and Beyond 157
One Final Thing to Consider 158

CHAPTER 1

Why Choose a Cockatiel?

Introduction

> *I would say that cockatiels are the best avian pet for first-time owners of parrots. Cockatiels are less moody than the larger parrot breeds, and they have an easier time getting along with other parrot breeds as well. They are not 'one-person' birds, so they can be close with every member of your family. They can mimic, learn tricks, and understand routine things just like the bigger birds, but they are kinder on your pocketbook. They are a lot of bang for your buck!*
>
> COLLEEN L. RIVAS
> *The Purple Parrot*

As pet owners, people tend to place themselves in categories. I'm a dog person. I'm a cat person. And you? You're an ornithophile—a fancy Greek word that simply means a person who loves birds. And as such, you've decided to get a cockatiel. Well, congratulations! You've chosen one of the best members of the parrot family to have. I can say from experience that these delightful birds become a part of the family. You'll know this when you realize some of the decisions the family makes revolve around the bird. Where's the best spot in the new house for

CHAPTER 1: Why Choose a Cockatiel?

their cage? What household cleaner is safe to purchase for use around the bird?

The good news is this book will help you navigate these questions and many more. But as far as being family pets, cockatiels are an excellent choice when looking for gentle, sweet-natured companions. We'll talk more about hand-fed babies later, but when cockatiels are bred in a loving, caring environment, they tend to bond quite naturally with their owners. They'll be happy to see you when you come home from work or school. They love to hang out while watching a movie and will even enjoy having you read a bedtime story to them. Plus, their small size is less intimidating for young children.

Taking care of one of these birds isn't hard, but it does require commitment, a commitment that involves patience and some self-sacrifice,

FUN FACT
Celebrity Cockatiel Owners

As an ornithophile, you're in good company. Many celebrities and important people own birds. Stephen Spielberg has a parrot. Paris Hilton owns an African Grey. And Steven Tyler keeps a Senegal parrot. Birds have even resided in the White House over the years. Many residents there have been bird lovers, including Dolly Madison, Theodore Roosevelt, and John F. Kennedy.

FUN FACT
Plenty of Shut-Eye

Cockatiels require a lot of sleep. These birds often enjoy upward of 14 hours of sleep per day.

especially in the beginning. Some people don't think about what it takes to raise one of these lovely creatures. My experience with our cockatiel, Sheldon, came to us because her original owner found she didn't want to take care of a bird after all. Like everything in life, it's not all fun and games, and when the cage had to be cleaned, fresh food prepared, vet visits made, and more, the woman found she didn't want to be a cockatiel owner after all. So, as you read on, weigh the facts and be sure the responsibility is one you're ready for. But overall, you don't have to be an expert aviculturist—another fancy word that simply means a person who keeps and breeds birds—to own a cockatiel. You just need to be a dedicated bird lover.

Basic Traits

> *Their size and gentle nature make them a good choice for children and first-time bird owners, and for experienced bird owners as well. Once they are comfortable with you, their personalities will shine—as will their love.*
>
> JESSICA OEGEMA
> *Casa la Parrot*

Cockatiels are laid-back, social birds, more so than many others. They're generally easygoing, but that doesn't mean they don't have their own personalities. You might be surprised to find one is a bit on the mischievous side and wants to be in the middle of everything the family is doing, while another may be more passive and prefer to chill by themselves. Keep this in mind when picking out your bird. In fact, I would

CHAPTER 1: Why Choose a Cockatiel?

advise drawing up a list of questions about the personality of the bird you're considering to be sure it's a good fit before making your purchase.

They're great for first-time bird owners because of the relative ease of care. Cockatiels make great little avian sidekicks. Some cockatiels can learn to repeat words and/or whistle. Actually, they can become exceptionally good whistlers. And when your cockatiel enjoys your company, the cockatiel may follow you around the house, do a dance for your attention, or serenade you for some praise.

Make sure you do some research to prepare yourself before you bring a cockatiel into your home. A cockatiel can seem noisy depending on your tolerance for noise. Do an online search for videos of cockatiels giving off

HISTORICAL FACT
Australian Natives

Cockatiels are native only to Australia and can often be found near bodies of water. These beautiful birds were discovered by European naturalists in the 18th century and became popular pets in the 20th century. Wild-caught cockatiels are no longer legal to own as pets, and as a result, all available cockatiels have been bred in captivity.

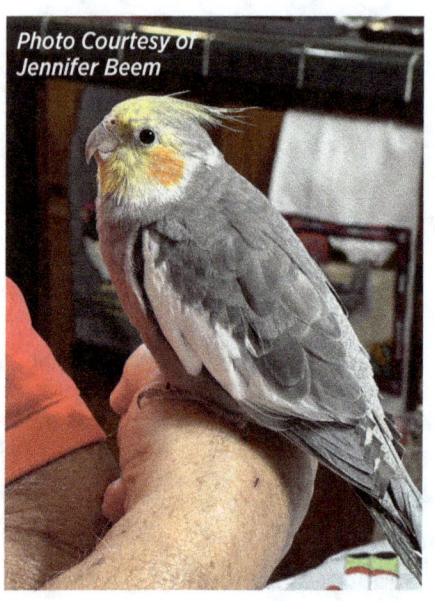

Photo Courtesy of Jennifer Beem

a flock call to learn their distinct vocalization. You should verify that you do not have allergies or a medical condition that could be affected by the cockatiel's dander. Cockatiels shed a lot of dander and dust. So, in the same way people can be allergic to cats, they can be allergic to cockatiels. Additionally, there's the life span. Experts say a cockatiel in captivity could live between 15 to 25 years, but some have been known to live 30+ years. Therefore, it's important to understand this and be prepared for a lifelong partnership with your bird.

Basic Anatomy

Cockatiels are the smallest of the cockatoo species. They only weigh about 3.5 ounces (100 grams). With slender bodies and long, pointed tails, they have a petite, delicate appearance about them. Though there are many types of cockatiels, they all have crests—a tufted array of feathers on top of the head. Cockatiels use their crests to communicate their feelings. Yes, they have feelings. They can experience emotions just like we do, and they will use their crests and body language to express many of those emotions. If a bird is upset, the cockatiel will flatten its crest to its head. However, when the bird is happy, it will still lay the crest flat, but the feathers will be relaxed, and the cheek

FUN FACT

Scottish naturalist Robert Kerr named the cockatiel Nymphicus hollandicus, after mythical nymphs. Nymphicus actually means little nymph.

CHAPTER 1: Why Choose a Cockatiel?

feathers will be slightly puffy. A sleepy cockatiel will hold the crest in a midway position. And when startled or frightened, the bird may point the crest straight up. So, take time to get to know your cockatiel's body language. Think how you would feel if you were angry or frightened and no one understood you.

Emotions cockatiels experience:

- Fear
- Happiness
- Anger
- Relaxation
- Contentment
- Curiosity

Photo Courtesy of Christina Conlin

As far as appearance, male and female cockatiels are very similar. This is something we discovered with Sheldon when he turned out to be Shelly. How did we learn the bird wasn't a male? One morning we found she'd laid an egg. It turns out that female cockatiels can lay an egg even if there is no male present. Never having had a male and female cockatiel at the same time, we didn't know what to look for in determining gender. However, in gray cockatiels, which is what we had, the male has yellow feathers that cover most of his face and head, including the crest, and each cheek has a bright orange patch on it. The female has some of the same coloring, but the colors are more muted. The yellow is mostly on the face and not the entire head, and the cheek patches are smaller and a duller shade of orange.

There will be some grooming tasks associated with having a cockatiel. Things like beaks, nails, feathers, and skin condition are important and will require attention from time to time. In the following chapters, we'll delve further into how to give your cockatiel a shower and what to do about nail overgrowth. And though the decision to clip a bird's wings is controversial, we'll look closer at it as well. The main thing to remember is a healthy, happy bird lives longer.

Color Varieties

The color of your cockatiel may be important to you, so you may want to consider color variations before taking that leap. Cockatiels are originally from Australia, and they were gray, literally called normal gray. But mutations came about through specific breeding, and the colors have evolved. There are now 18+ different color variations available for consideration. Pearl cockatiels are known for the beautiful white lacy markings across their plumage. White-faced cockatiels are just that, white-faced. They lack the bright yellow feathers and orange patches normal grays have. Blue cockatiels aren't actually blue. Like White-faced cockatiels, Blues don't have yellow cheeks and orange patches, but their wingtips are a dark gray, and the shades of blue are on their gray tails.

Boutin's Journal

My granddaughter had a cockatiel named Polly. Every morning when she watched SpongeBob SquarePants, Polly joined her, squawking with the seagulls in the theme song.

CHAPTER 1: Why Choose a Cockatiel?

It's understandable to have a color preference, but you can take comfort in knowing a cockatiel's color doesn't affect its temperament or its health. They're warm and friendly birds, no matter the color.

CHAPTER 2

The History of Cockatiels

History

With the ability to hop on a plane and be across the country in a matter of hours, or with the simple click of a button to order a product from another country that will arrive in only days, it's easy to forget the world hasn't always been this small. But there was a time when cockatiels weren't so readily available.

CHAPTER 2: The History of Cockatiels

Cockatiels are native to the Australian Outback, a region in the northern part of the continent down under. And we can thank British explorer James Cook for bringing them to the world's attention. The naval captain was an explorer and cartographer who made three Pacific Ocean expeditions, one of which was on the HMS Endeavor and included stops in Australia. Considered one of the greatest navigators of all time, he's a celebrated British hero. He mapped the east coast of Australia and made way for British settlement 18 years later.

Captain Cook's voyages were known to bring back specimens of birds, and it was on his 1770 voyage that he is believed to have discovered the cockatiel and brought one home with him to Europe. By the 1900s, cockatiels had become popular as pets. They're easy to breed in captivity, and their docile, friendly nature makes them ideal for home life. Thankfully, it's now easy to purchase a cockatiel because the birds can no longer be trapped or exported from Australia.

In the Wild

These birds still survive in the wilds of Australia. Although some are found in Tasmania, they were most likely introduced by humans. You may be wondering why it matters where cockatiels originated if you're buying yours from a local breeder or pet shop. It's always wise to know how any pet lives in the wild in order to provide the best care for it at home. There's mixed opinion on whether the cockatiel is considered domesticated or not, but regardless, a pet cockatiel will act much like its wild counterpart. The color mutations previously mentioned have no bearing on the bird's behavior. Nonetheless, it will help you to be a better

CHAPTER 2: The History of Cockatiels

owner if you understand some of the traits they've developed over the evolution of the species. Here are a few insights about your bird's innate habits and mannerisms.

Habitat

In the arid, desert-like Australian Outback, cockatiels will be found near a water source because they need a lot to survive. They tend to prefer open areas with a few trees for nesting. Those nests are usually in cavities in the trees—spaces hollowed out by other animals. (Seems pretty smart to get someone else to do the work for you, don't you think?)

Diet

Wild cockatiels exert more energy than pet cockatiels and consequently need more food. Rather than a pointed beak, the wild cockatiel developed a curved beak, perfect for foraging seeds and grains that were available in Australia. For the most part, they're herbivores, but sometimes cockatiels eat insects. Unfortunately, they've been known to raid farmers' crops, leaving the farmers none too happy. But another thing they learned to do with those fabulous beaks in the wild is to use them as a climbing tool. So, if you see your bird using his beak to scale his cage or even your sofa, this is a trait developed from living in the wild.

DID YOU KNOW?
Cockatiel Longevity

Cockatiels typically survive around 10 years in the wild and live between 16 to 25 years in captivity. According to Guinness World Records, the oldest cockatiel, named Sunshine, was 32 years old in January 2016. Sunshine was purchased in Colorado in 1983 and made multiple moves with his owner, Vickie Aranda, during his life. Other reports indicate that the oldest cockatiel lived to be 36 years old in captivity.

Socializing

Cockatiels are nomads. And though that may seem like a solitary life, it's quite the opposite for them. These birds are highly sociable animals who live and travel in flocks, and a single flock can have hundreds of cockatiels. When food and water supplies begin to run low, they simply move as a flock to find more. It's a family affair, and they pal around together in the morning, singing and then moving to the ground to look for seeds. Mates within the flock groom each other, pruning their heads and crests, which means, as a flock family member, you will likely be preened too!

Longevity

As stated before, pet cockatiels can live 15 to 25 years, but the life expectancy for one in the wild is much less. It's closer to 10 years for

CHAPTER 2: The History of Cockatiels

them. Cockatiels are prey animals. They're mostly hunted by larger birds like hawks and eagles. As a result, they've developed some behaviors as defense mechanisms. For instance, if sick, they sometimes won't show it until the illness is advanced. They can't afford to appear as easy targets for predators. This is something to be aware of in your pet. They also have loud, shrill vocalizations used as warning alarms. They'll screech and flap their wings to ward off a perceived threat, and they can fly up to 40 miles an hour to escape a predator.

Remember, when you first get your new friend, he's not going to know you. And even if you've spent time bonding with him at the breeder's, he still won't know his new home and surrounding atmosphere. Instinct lies just beneath the surface of his beautiful feathers, and he will naturally be in survival mode. So, it's good to know what to expect and how to recognize behavior that may need addressing. We'll talk more about mitigating some of your cockatiel's worries and fears in the coming chapters.

Photo Courtesy of Cozzi Larsen

Male cockatiels are exceptional fathers. They're nurturing and affectionate and will face down much larger birds to protect their young.

CHAPTER 3

Where to Get Your Cockatiel

Now that you've decided to get a cockatiel, the questions are where and from whom? In this chapter, we're going to look at the various options out there. You may be surprised to learn how many there are. We will be considering big-chain pet stores, exotic bird and pet stores, commercial breeders, bird shows, and rescue adoptions. It's important to avoid an impulse buy before educating yourself. Be prepared with the facts. If not, you could easily find yourself falling in love with a sick bird who might not survive.

Before we dig into these different purchasing options, see what **William Dodson of Tiel Hill Aviaries** advises when starting your search for a cockatiel.

> *The first step to choosing where to get a cockatiel from is knowing who tests for diseases (and what diseases). Bacterial infections (i.e., Bordetella) can be passed from bird to bird and may not show up at first. Sellers that offer 'vet-checked' birds are not a bypass of disease testing. Generally, breeders of quality cockatiels will have disease-testing records ... do not be afraid to ask breeders what diseases they test for and how they test. Going through a breeder can usually save a little bit of money, but it really depends on the situation. A breeder is definitely more knowledgeable than a person working in a pet store when it comes to the details of keeping cockatiels.*

CHAPTER 3: Where to Get Your Cockatiel

Chain Pet Stores

Pet stores come to mind first as an easy solution for finding a cockatiel. Big-chain pet stores can be found in most major cities. There are, however, some drawbacks with big-chain pet stores. If you've ever been in one, you know they sell a wide variety of animals. They don't specialize in birds. Employees may not be trained as to what to look for in a bird's health and well-being. Birds in pet stores can be prone to respiratory disease and may even carry those respiratory infections for months before they're discovered. Chain pet store birds are also going to be more expensive. That's because the store bought them from a breeder and consequently has to raise the price to make a profit.

This is not to say that there aren't perfectly good chain stores from which you can buy your bird. And there are some things you can look for when making your decision. The first and most obvious would be the condition of the cage. Is it clean? Is there overcrowding of the birds? Do the birds appear alert and interactive? It's not a good sign if a bird is listless and sitting on the bottom of the cage. The bird's eyes should be clear, and its feathers should be smooth and not puffed up. Further, its cloaca, the opening for its urinary, intestinal, and reproductive tracts found under the base of the tail, should be clean as well.

Photo Courtesy of Tiffany Shorey

Additionally, it's crucial to hold the bird. If it acts wild and fearful, that's a clue it might not have been trained and socialized, possibly even parent-raised. (Think about those behaviors learned in the wild discussed in Chapter 2.) If it hisses at you and/or tries to bite you, that's another good indicator that the bird may not be tame. Also, you want to be sure the bird was properly weaned and hand-fed—no forced weaning. That's when handheld food is withheld in

Photo Courtesy of Michelle Crawford

an attempt to get the bird to eat on its own. This can lead to behavioral problems.

The majority of breeders and professional bird handlers don't recommend buying a bird from a big-chain store. But if this is your only option, be sure to check reviews of the store. Remember, you're the customer. This puts you in the driver's seat, so don't be afraid to ask questions and request health records, lineage, and the like. You don't want your cockatiel to have been raised in a bird mill where the breeders don't care for or interact with the birds because their only interest is in the sale. If the store can't or won't answer your questions, you may want to reconsider purchasing your cockatiel there.

Exotic Bird and Pet Stores

Exotic bird and pet stores are another option when looking to purchase a cockatiel. Often these establishments are smaller, family-owned businesses, and they tend to have been around for years, supplying healthier exotic pets than chain stores do. Employees at these stores are sometimes more informed, passionate about birds, and inclined to handle and interact with them, ensuring the birds' socialization. These stores may buy their birds from breeders the same way chain stores do, but they're more likely to have an established, ongoing relationship with the breeder. What's more, some of these stores breed their own birds, ensuring your bird has a well-rounded upbringing.

CHAPTER 3: Where to Get Your Cockatiel

Jessica Oegema at Casa la Parrot gives this advice when preparing to buy a cockatiel:

> *Starting with a hand-fed baby will get you the best result. Reputable breeders and bird-focused pet stores are more likely to have hand-fed babies. Picking out a baby and visiting it often while it is still learning to eat on its own is a great way to start forming a bond between you and your bird before your bird goes home.*

Frequently, these mom-and-pop stores offer more than a simple sale. They can walk you through the process of adapting to being a new bird owner. They can educate you about food, even supply it, address health concerns, and answer any other questions you might have. Many of these stores offer services beyond the sale, like trimming, boarding, and even veterinary services. A small store like this can be a valuable resource long after you've taken your bird home. Don't be afraid to establish a rapport with them. After all, you're going to have your cockatiel for many years to come.

Boutin's Journal

I find these small, privately owned stores to be my personal preference. Not only does my family own birds, but as a writer, I've done research on macaws for a couple of works of fiction at one of these shops.

Commercial Breeders

> *Big pet stores generally aren't very knowledgeable about bird care. It's usually younger kids who are working there, and the turnover rate is high. Breeders spend more time with their babies and have a much better understanding of what it takes to care for cockatiels. A good breeder will also be available for questions after you take your baby home, and pet stores usually don't offer that benefit.*
>
> LISA SZUMITA
> Utah Parrots

A simple internet search will help you locate local bird breeders. They can be found on Google and through online marketplaces like Craigslist and Facebook Marketplace. As recommended before, do your research. Reputable breeders will likely have an online presence and may have

CHAPTER 3: Where to Get Your Cockatiel

references and testimonials available on their websites. Ideally, you should be able to contact owners who have bought birds from the breeder. Firsthand testimonials are the best. Something else to look for is their reputation in the bird-breeding world. Have they won any awards, maybe at bird shows?

Commercial breeders tend to care more about their birds. They've often gotten into the business out of a love for the creatures and not just to make money. Concern for their birds' welfare comes before profits. They spend time with their birds because they want to. They hand feed and handle them to start them off as affectionate pets. And like exotic pet stores, they will be there for you in the years to come, ready to help. As far as choices, commercial breeders will many times have more mutations, meaning all sorts of amazing colors to choose from. Plus, you can trace your bird's lineage and genetics through a breeder—in case you want to breed your bird.

It is not advised that you buy your bird and have him shipped to you in a box through a postal service. Shipping a bird is extremely stressful for your pet. They may stop eating, and birds who only weigh three ounces can't afford to lose weight. The stress can compromise their immune

HELPFUL TIP

National Cockatiel Society (NCS)

Established in 1983, the National Cockatiel Society (NCS) strives to educate its members, support responsible breeding, and further research into cockatiel health issues and nutrition. The NCS publishes a quarterly journal for members and hosts annual nationwide exhibitions. In addition, the NCS maintains a list of registered aviaries on its website, listed by state. For more information about this society or affiliated clubs, visit www.ncscockatiels.org.

system, making them vulnerable to illness. A shipping box is not going to be a particularly hygienic place for your bird to stay for any length of time, and it could develop a staph infection. The stress can cause other undesirable behaviors like feather plucking, when birds pluck their feathers from their skin, leaving them naked and exposed to the elements. These are just a few reasons why shipping a bird is ill-advised. There are some breeders, such as Lisa Szumita of Utah Parrots who will ship their birds in modified cages using airlines to transport them. This can eliminate many of the issues of prolonged travel and result in a much less stressful move for your Cockatiel.

Bird Shows

Aside from the possibility of buying your cockatiel at a bird show, bird shows are a great place to start your research before making that purchase. Like any other convention or fair, bird shows are filled with merchandise, educational materials, people devoted to their work, and pretty much anything else associated with birds. This is the place to have all your questions answered. It's also a great way to meet other cockatiel owners and aficionados and become a part of their flock. (Pun totally intended.) You can make connections that will extend beyond the event and maybe join online groups to keep in touch. It's also a way to get the latest news on the latest products, even to have discussions about some of the stickier issues of owning a cockatiel, like clipping the bird's wings.

CHAPTER 3: Where to Get Your Cockatiel

Moreover, this is where you can meet some breeders and get to know them. A number of these events hold competitions. This puts you in a position to learn what to look for in your own bird by meeting the breeders. It's a good time to interview them, so to speak, to get a feel for how they are with their birds. And though you can certainly buy your bird from one of the vendors at the convention, you may want to make a list of your favorites, and then, after the show is over, visit these different breeders and make your decision. For the most part, these shows and conventions are inexpensive. You can usually get in for less than $10, and kids' entry is even free in some cases.

Resources

- The National Cockatiel Society: www.ncscockatiels.org
- St. Augustine Bird Expo: https://www.staugustineexoticbirdfair.com
- Acadian Bird Fair and Sale: https://www.acadianabirdclubinc.com/acadiana-bird-fair
- Idaho Pet Expo: https://www.iblevents.com/family-pet-expo
- Verde Valley Birding and Nature Festival: https://verderiver.org/birding-festival/

You may not live in an area close to one of these bird shows, so here's the next best thing. The people at Parrot Fun Zone have created an entertaining and educational website for the whole family. There are interactive parrot-themed games like jigsaw puzzles, memory games, and my favorite, JeopBirdy! It's Jeopardy with bird facts. And it's hard. But fun. There are tons of things to explore there—bird videos, recipes, and full-color downloadable activity books. I highly recommend you go hang out and play for a while.
www.parrotfunzone.com

Adopting from Local Shelters and Rescues

Some people prefer to adopt an animal rather than buy it from a store, and this is certainly an option with cockatiels. Owning a cockatiel is a decades-long commitment, and sometimes people find their life's

Photo Courtesy of Gary Peterford

CHAPTER 3: Where to Get Your Cockatiel

circumstances make this no longer possible. After my grandmother passed away, her cockatiel, Pepper, came to live with my family. Had we not been able to take him in, he would likely have been sent to a rescue. There are many reasons why birds might end up in a rescue, but as they are wonderfully affectionate animals, they can still make absolutely marvelous pets.

There are many shelters and rescues, and a simple internet search can bring up a list of rescues and shelters that may have pet cockatiels up for adoption in your area. Many of these establishments are 501c3 nonprofit organizations dedicated to providing safe places for surrendered birds to live, giving them time to be adopted or fostered into new homes. These rescues and shelters may have an adoption process or adoption fee. They do this to make sure the adopters are serious about adoption and understand the care for these cockatiels. The rescues and shelters have these processes in place in trying to reduce the cockatiel being rehomed again.

Cockatiels that are up for adoption are not damaged or have baggage. They are wonderful birds that need the right person to understand their behavior and give them the proper care.

Further, some of the privately owned exotic bird and pet shops previously mentioned also provide rescue and adoption services. Many of them have rehoming programs. So, if it's in your heart to offer a home to a bird who may have lost his beloved family for one reason or another, this is a thoughtful and kind way to do it.

Resources for Adopting

Petfinder: https://www.petfinder.com/
ASPCA: https://www.aspca.org
Humane Society: https://www.humanesociety.org

CHAPTER 4

How to Choose Your Cockatiel

Choose Wisely

> *When picking out your cockatiel, take your time and let the bird 'choose' you. Picking out a baby and visiting it often while it is still learning to eat on its own is a great way to start forming a bond between you and your bird before it comes home with you.*
>
> JESSICA OEGEMA
> *Casa la Parrot*

In this chapter, we're going to unpack some of the things we touched on when it comes to choosing your bird. This is an important decision because you will be responsible for its life for a very long time. I don't want to say it's akin to having a child, but in all honesty, it's at least an equal responsibility. Think about it. A child grows and learns to do things for itself—walk, eat, go to school, and get a job! But with a cockatiel, you will be feeding it, cleaning it, taking it to the doctor, nursing it when it's sick, etc., for years to come. So, getting a bird shouldn't be a form of "retail therapy."

Author's Advice:

This might seem obvious, but don't buy a bird from a flea market. My niece did this because it was cheaper, and her bird died not long after. You don't save money when you don't choose wisely. Birds in these places are continually traumatized. They're transported and moved around frequently, squeezed into cages with too many other birds, fed cheap diets, and stressed beyond their ability to cope. Spend a few dollars more and find a reputable venue to buy your companion. Plus, if people stop buying birds from these vendors, they'll stop selling them and thereby stop abusing them.

Hand-fed Birds

We mentioned this earlier, but let's take a closer look at the importance of considering hand-fed babies. First off, you should never take an unweaned cockatiel home. Weaning should be done by an experienced professional. Hand feeding is time-consuming, as well as a bonding experience. It can cause behavioral problems early on in the bird's development if not done right, problems that continue into the bird's adult life.

Likewise, you don't want a bird that is force weaned. This is when the bird is taken off the formula before it's ready. The bird shouldn't

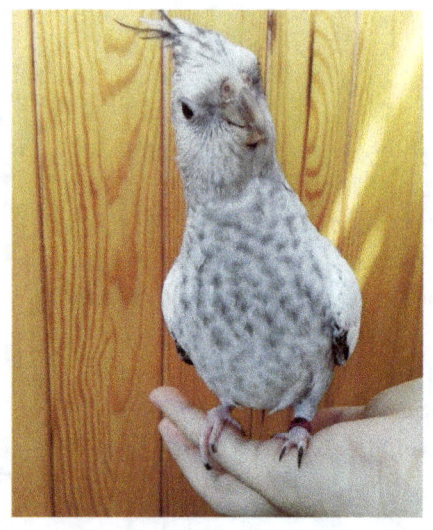

be expected to eat solid food just because it's hungry any more than a baby would be expected to spontaneously eat solid food by being deprived of milk. Forced weaning is detrimental, so be sure to ask about the type of weaning used in raising the bird.

The benefits of hand feeding, beyond the obvious of the bird being handled, are also how it affects the bird psychologically. Birds that receive abundance weaning—augmenting formula by adding/introducing other foods—are more sociable, docile, and friendly. This is something to think about when checking out pet stores. In a chain store, the birds can be handled by different employees or left to sit in cages with little to no interaction. And ultimately, when choosing your cockatiel, you want it to have had the best start in life possible.

> *A well-raised, hand-fed baby will not be biting the breeder or workers.*
>
> LISA SZUMITA
> *Utah Parrots*

Signs and Clues to Look For in a Store or Breeder

This step requires a combination of your sense of sight and intuition. Starting with what you see, the cages should be clean with no droppings dried on the grating. The water bowl should have clean, clear water in it. Is there overcrowding in the cage? Crowding causes stress, which can lead to aggression and territorialism.

This is why most experts don't recommend chain stores. That, and if you use a breeder or small exotic pet store, many of them will let you pick out your bird as a baby and visit regularly. If you're there when it's being fed and learning to eat on its own, that time spent with it will start that bond you want. It gives you a head start before bringing your baby home.

Here are some suggested questions for a potential breeder or store

- What diet has the bird been on? (It's recommended you continue that diet until the bird has adjusted to the new home.)
- Where do you get your birds? (If not a breeder)
- Is there a warranty? (This may sound strange, but you're investing a lot of money in your cockatiel and everything it takes to give it a

home. And since birds can carry undetected illnesses, you don't want to bring a cockatiel home and have something unthinkable happen.)
- Do you have any references?
- How have you socialized the bird?
- Has the bird been vetted for diseases? (Ask to see the documentation of the veterinary exams, including blood work)
- Review the leg band. (You might be able to look for information based on the leg band.)

> *Be sure to check out the breeder, his aviary or cages, his references or reputation, and actually hold the bird to be sure it is unafraid, tame, and socialized.*
>
> BRIDGET MARQUEZ
> *Marquez Tiels*

CHAPTER 4: How to Choose Your Cockatiel

Individual Bird

> *Always be sure to actually hold a bird you are considering to be sure it is unafraid, tame, and socialized. If the bird tries to bite you and hisses, it is not tame and socialized. Its eyes should be clear, its feathers smooth and not puffed up, and its vent and cage should be clean. Never buy a bird that lacks energy or sits at the bottom of its cage.*
>
> BRIDGET MARQUEZ
> *Marquez Tiels*

As you consider purchasing your cockatiel, you'll probably be inclined to think about its appearance when making your decision, but try to be open to the bird's personality when doing so. Each cockatiel is unique,

Photo Courtesy of Emily Rinearson

and experts will tell you the birds are known for "choosing" their human. That's why it's helpful to visit (another benefit of using a breeder or individually owned store) more than once. This gives you, as well as the bird, time to get to know each other. If you're looking for a cuddly sweetheart who just likes to snuggle, you might not want to bring home a hyperactive attention-seeker just because it's a pearl cockatiel with beautiful lacy designs.

More importantly, though, looking for a healthy bird should be your priority. We'll get into this more later, but here's a list of things to consider the minute you step into the store.

8 Signs a Cockatiel Is Healthy

1. Alert and bright-eyed
2. Clean, shiny feathers
3. Healthy droppings should be black or solid dark green, with a clear portion and a creamy white portion
4. Good appetite and lots of energy
5. Aware and watchful of their surroundings, upright on their perches, balanced, and quite active
6. Clear nostrils
7. Steady and quiet breathing
8. A smooth beak with no growths, rough spots, or peeling.

8 Signs a Cockatiel Is Unhealthy

1. Fluffed feathers (it looks fatter)
2. Standing on two feet with eyes closed (they usually stand on one foot)
3. Eyes are red, swollen, cloudy, or have discharge
4. Nasal discharge or blockage
5. Tail feathers that don't bob when the bird is breathing
6. Bleeding or trauma to the body
7. Wet droppings or diarrhea
8. Balance difficulties

CHAPTER 4: How to Choose Your Cockatiel

Should You Get a Male or Female Cockatiel?

> *A cockatiel can reach a vocabulary of over 200 words. At the age of one, they can usually learn about 50 words. Although males usually can learn to mimic easier than females, it doesn't mean that females can't mimic at all.*
>
> COLLEEN L. RIVAS
> *The Purple Parrot*

If you're obtaining a cockatiel simply as a companion bird and not necessarily for breeding, the sex of the bird may not matter to you. And you can be sure the sex has no effect on their nature. Males and females alike are friendly, affectionate birds. You can have a loving, enduring relationship with either one. The differences between the two genders are subtle. When they're babies, it's almost impossible to tell because their plumage has yet to fill in. Sometimes a DNA test has to be done to learn the sex. However, there are a few things to watch for when determining gender. But be aware these are not hard and fast rules.

Males tend to have richer, more vibrant coloration. This is because they use their brilliant plumage to attract a mate. Though they both have some mixture of gray and yellow, the males will have brighter shades of yellow, and the females will have more muted grays.

Cockatiels are songbirds, males in particular. Along with their appearance, they use their voices to attract a female, singing them love songs, if you will. As the more vociferous of the two, males tend to mimic

The orange patches beneath a cockatiel's eyes are called cheddar cheeks.

and learn human speech easier than females do. Though there can be exceptions, in general, the male courts the female using his good looks, captivating song, and lively jig. That doesn't mean that a female might not enjoy singing and doing a dance for you, though. Again, there are no strict guidelines here.

Another way to tell a bird's gender is by its parentage. That's because there are sex-linked mutations associated with the parents' coloring. Certain colors will only be passed down to certain sexes. So, if the gender of your cockatiel is important to you, you may want to buy it from a breeder. They'll have more experience with the process and know the parents the bird came from.

Comparison of Male and Female Cockatiels

♂	♀
Vibrant colors	Muted colors
Melodic singing	Quieter
May learn tricks more easily	More docile

One Bird or Two?

Recall that in the wild, cockatiels live in flocks, some of them quite large, so they're not solitary by nature. They thrive with a companion and mate for life. However, that doesn't mean your bird can't do just as well with you as its companion. A single cockatiel can live happily in such an environment. That said, if you will be gone for extended periods of time—work, travel, etc.—your bird will suffer emotionally from the lack of interaction. You don't want your bird to become distressed, so in a case like this, you might consider having a second cockatiel.

CHAPTER 4: How to Choose Your Cockatiel

> *I highly recommend keeping only one cockatiel per cage. While it is possible for them to stay friendly to humans in pairs, it is extremely difficult (and not guaranteed). They are far more likely to bond to each other, rather than to you, if they share the same space for most of the day. It is much easier to keep your bird friendly when you don't need to compete for its attention with another bird.*
>
> JESSICA OEGEMA
> Casa la Parrot

Alternative Viewpoint

"I've always, even when I first had cockatiels in 1993, kept more than one in a cage and they have always been just as sweet. I've had several people get more than one from and have never had an issue with tameness or sweetness. Cockatiels are one of the few birds you can do that with. Make note that this is with 'non-breeding' pairs, those can be all together different." **Lisa Szumita – Utah Parrots**

Warning Signs Your Bird Is Suffering from Stress

Feather picking or self-harm: This is exactly what it sounds like. Trauma can cause a bird to pluck its own feathers—and so can isolation. Birds may even begin chewing and biting their own skin. This behavior can continue even when the situation has been resolved. With medical assistance and behavior training, these situations can be reduced. The sooner you see this behavior, the better chance of reducing the behavior.

Stress bars: These are visible, horizontal lines that run across a bird's feathers, usually the tail feathers. They can be caused by many things, like poor nutrition and stressful situations, including being alone for extended periods of time. As the feathers grow, stress bars are formed as a result of the stress they experienced. If left untreated, stress bars can lead to skin damage and even feather plucking and self-harm.

Loss of appetite: If your bird suddenly starts eating less, this can be a sign of stress or other health problems. It's advised that you see an avian vet to rule out health problems, and then, by process of elimination—the cage was relocated; there's a new person in the home; the bird was left alone too long—you can figure out what is causing this conduct.

Aggression: If your cockatiel is normally docile and affectionate and unexpectedly starts hissing, lunging, or screaming and screeching, it could be the stress.

Changes in Vocalization: Cockatiels tend to be pretty vocal, and occasional loud noises are normal, but if your bird appears overly intentional with its screaming and screeching, it may be a sign of stress, illness, or boredom. At the same time, some cockatiels may do the opposite and lessen their vocalizations when unhappy. It depends on the individual bird.

Fear: This is when your normally content bird acts afraid of you or other family members who it's usually comfortable around. This doesn't

---

FUN FACT
Cockatiel Color Mutations

Due to selective breeding and inherited color mutations, cockatiels are available in various colors. The typical cockatiel coloring consists of a gray body, a yellow head, and white markings on the edges of the wings. As of 2023, there are approximately 18 different cockatiel color mutations, including lutino, cinnamon, silver, albino, and olive. The white-faced cockatiel mutation is possibly the rarest mutation and results in a bird with a white or grayish face without any yellow or orange plumage. It's unclear whether color mutations affect a cockatiel's personality or disposition.

Photo Courtesy of Corrie Cowger

necessarily mean the person is directly causing a problem. Rather, it could be triggered by something as simple as the color of a person's clothing or something or someone new brought into the bird's environment, including another bird.

Boredom: Cockatiels are highly intelligent, energetic birds. They need stimulation. We'll cover enrichment activities later in the book, but suffice it to say a lack of mental stimulus can affect your cockatiel's overall health and well-being.

If your bird exhibits any of these behaviors, take it to the vet as soon as possible. Cockatiel experts recommend an avian vet because they specialize in birds. Your cockatiel is not a mammal. The cockatiels care will be different from that of a cat or dog. Also, there are some things you can do to ease your bird's trauma until you can get it to the vet. You can start by reducing noise. For the bird, loud noises are a sign of danger. Then there's the cage. If the cockatiel is reacting to a change in its cage's placement—maybe you've moved it, whether to a different room or different home—cover the cage with a sheet, then gradually uncover it over time so the bird can adjust to the new placement. If boredom is the problem, give your pet plenty of things to do. You can rearrange objects in the cage and add lots of bird-safe toys. And, of course, make sure it is getting enough food.

The Decision Is Subjective

As you can see, there is no straightforward answer to this question. A single cockatiel can suffer stress when left home alone for extended periods of time. Likewise, introducing a new bird to the home can cause trauma. Oddly enough, like humans, some cockatiels do better in pairs, while others don't. They are individuals with their own temperaments. Something else to consider—with just two birds, they could bond and completely leave you out of the picture. Or they may both love you. It could easily go either way. There's really no way of knowing how multiple cockatiels will react when put together.

The answer to the question one bird or two comes down to what you want from the experience. Are you willing to put in the work and added expense of having multiple birds? Can you invest your time in acclimating the birds? What about the clean-up? Food preparation? Vet visits? Hopefully, you can take the information laid out here, weigh it with your own intentions, and make a decision you and your bird(s) will be happy with for years to come.

CHAPTER 5

Creating a Home

Welcoming Your Cockatiel Home

> *When young birds are first taken to their new home, they can exhibit some behaviors that they will outgrow, but they can be concerning for new owners. Keep in mind that everything they've known up to this point in their life has changed. There are new sights, sounds, smells, and people. Just be patient and remember that they've had a major life change, but with a bit of time, they should come out of it quickly.*
>
> DANA GRIMM
> *Beaks and Tweets Aviary*

With any luck, you've learned enough now to know who you want to buy your cockatiel from, as well as what to look for in the bird itself. Now it's time to ready your home and create a safe and welcoming place for your cockatiel. Ideally, you want this done before buying the bird. This environment will all be new to him or her, and we already know change can be stressful for cockatiels. The more you can do to make this transition smoother for your bird, the better. Your new pet will have an easier time adjusting if what it needs is already in place when it arrives.

In this chapter, we'll get into the details of how to choose a cage along with other paraphernalia, but let's talk about those first few hours you have your bird at home. Even if you were fortunate enough to bond with

CHAPTER 5: Creating a Home

your cockatiel at the breeder's, it still might undergo discomfort in its new cage. It's best to put it in the cage and simply leave it alone. You can sit in the same room as the cockatiel (but give it some space), quietly passing the time and just being yourself. This allows the bird the opportunity to

Photo Courtesy of Jennifer White

acclimate to the new smells and sounds of its surroundings and see that you're not afraid, so it doesn't need to be afraid either.

If you have other animals, it's wise to keep them away from the room the cockatiel is in for a time. Allow the bird to adapt to the new space anywhere from two weeks to a month. Then slowly introduce the other pets, and never with the bird out of its cage. Just as it is recommended that you sit by the cage and spend time with the bird without forcing interaction, your other animals can be introduced in the same way. Hold your pet and calmly sit with it next to the cage. And remember, a cockatiel is a prey species, so it will naturally be afraid of animals it doesn't know, especially dogs and cats, which are predatory species. Even if the animal is merely curious, exhibiting natural behaviors like swatting and slapping could hurt the bird. Above all, think about safety. Make sure the cockatiel's cage is secure and no other animal can get to the bird inside. Again, never let it out of the cage with other predatory-by-nature pets in the same room.

Another thing to be aware of when you bring your new cockatiel home is that the bird may not eat for several hours, maybe the whole day. This is normal. If the bird goes beyond that, then seek professional help. This is why it's good to have built a relationship with the breeder or find support before you get the cockatiel, someone you can reach out to with questions in those first few days.

It will take a couple of weeks for your cockatiel to become accustomed to its new home, but the bird will eventually relax and begin to reveal its personality to you. Then the bird will likely become curious and maybe a little naughty, which is when the fun begins. (wink-wink)

> *When you bring a new bird home, you should have a point of contact for all the questions you will come across. (This is another benefit of buying from a breeder and not a store.) When you ask that trusted and experienced person, do what they say. Do not Google or take it to Facebook for everyone's opinion.*
>
> WILLIAM DODSON
> *Tiel Hill Aviaries*

CHAPTER 5: Creating a Home

The Right Cage

> *Please provide the largest cage that space and money can afford. Cockatiels have long crests and tails, and the cage must accommodate this. The cage for a sole cockatiel must be at least three times its tail length and three times its wingspan. A flight cage is recommended, and you must NEVER put your bird in a round or cornerless cage.*
>
> BRIDGET MARQUEZ
> *Marquez Tiels*

Things are getting exciting now. You're ready to pick out your cockatiel's cage and all the fun stuff that goes along with it. But which cage do you choose? Is bigger better? Minimal versus the works? How about a pretty round cage? Let's take a look at some of the options and weigh the pros and cons.

To begin with, the best cages are made of stainless steel. They're non-toxic and won't rust, so they won't harm your bird. Stainless steel is easy to clean and won't chip; it's sturdy and holds up well, and since this could be your cockatiel's forever home, it should be the safest environment possible.

Photo Courtesy of Taria Smith

As to size, you don't want one of the small display-style cages used in pet stores. Those are for exhibition only. Many experts recommend a flight cage. Flight cages are usually bigger than ordinary cages and give your cockatiel plenty of room for executing more than a few flaps of its wings at a

Photo Courtesy of Jen Thomas

time. A good guideline is to buy a cage that is three times the length of the bird's wingspan, that is, from the tip of one wing to the tip of the other. Birds don't fly up and down; rather, they fly horizontally. So, they need a wide space to get proper exercise.

What's more, if you decide to buy two birds and plan to house them together, you will need a cage large enough for two birds to fly around in. Or, since you won't know how well these two cockatiels will cohabitate, you may want two cages. This is an added cost, so be sure you've thought through what is required for caring for multiple cockatiels.

If you're fortunate enough to have a room where your bird can fly free, it's possible to have a smaller ordinary cage as a home base for the bird. But if your bird will be in the cage for long periods of time, you'll need one large enough to accommodate a healthy lifestyle for your friend.

Buying a Cage by the Numbers

- Three times the average wingspan of 10 to 12 inches (double if for two birds)
- Three times the average tail length of 12 inches
- 1/2- to 5/8-inch horizontal bar spacing

> "We recommend 36" x 24" x 66" for a pair of cockatiels."
>
> BRIDGET MARQUEZ
> Marquez Tiels

CHAPTER 5: Creating a Home

Round Cages

It's generally recommended you not buy a round cage. There are a lot of opinions about how a round cage affects a bird psychologically. Some say it's emotionally distressing for the bird and can cause unwanted behavior. The goal here is not to debate these opinions but to take a look at the features and compare round to rectangular or square cages to determine which is best for the cockatiel.

First, the round shape causes your bird's feathers to come in contact with the bars more frequently, and this can damage the feathers. It will wear them down and make them appear battered. This is especially true if you have more than one bird in the cage.

Second, because most cages nowadays are square or rectangular, it can be difficult to find accessories that fit a round cage well. Many accessories have double clips and are made to fit a rectangle or square cage where the bars are equal lengths apart.

Third, round cages can be difficult to clean. The entire top has to be taken off to reach the bottom, where the bedding or paper liner is. This isn't fun. Also, it's difficult to clean between the bars where they narrow and come together. Most square and rectangular cages have removable substrate grates and trays, making cleaning much easier.

Finally, and most importantly, round cages are dangerous. A round cage's construction causes the bars to narrow where the cage comes together at the top. This can lead to wings, feet, or legs getting caught, any of which could easily be broken. So, the number one reason for not getting a round cage is your sweet pet's safety.

Photo Courtesy of Rosa al-Herbawi

New or Used?

So far, everything discussed is adding up. Consequently, you may want to find a way to save some money, and the cage, being the most expensive element aside from the cockatiel itself, might be your first thought. Besides all the safety issues we've mentioned in this chapter, there are a few other things to think about before buying a used cage.

- Don't buy the cage sight unseen because it's important to do a full inspection of it. Are there any bent or broken bars? Has the cage been altered in any way? Is there rust and/or chips on it?
- Is the cage old, possibly making its construction outdated and dangerous?
- Ask what happened to the bird that lived in it before. If that bird died from a communicable disease, the germs can be left behind in the cage. Yes, you can clean the cage, and if you do, you want to be thorough with it. A cup of bleach can be added to a gallon of water to spray the entire cage. Be sure to scrub cracks, crevices, and tiny corners where germs can hide. Remember, bleach is toxic for

CHAPTER 5: Creating a Home

your bird. Make sure you have rinsed the cage well, and then rinse it again. Finally, rinse it once more. And, of course, don't have your bird in the vicinity, as the fumes are dangerous for its tiny lungs.

Buying a used cage is certainly an option. Just be sure to take every precaution you can to keep your cockatiel safe.

Cockatiels are messy eaters.

So, to cut back on some of the bird confetti (my word for the mixture of seeds, feathers, and dander that results from having a cockatiel), consider buying a cage skirt. Cage skirts fit around the bottom half of the cage to hold in some of the stray confetti that floats to the floor. Most cage skirts are made of mesh and are held up by an elastic band. You can get fancy, though, and find custom-made skirts on the internet.

Cage Placement

> *If you feel that the room is cold, you can place your cockatiel under a heat lamp or near a sunlit window (you should never attempt to warm it with a blow dryer, though!) They require natural sunlight on a daily basis—and not sunlight filtered through glass. An avian lamp can do the job if no windows are available.*
>
> BRIDGET MARQUEZ
> *Marquez Tiels*

Choosing the right room for your cockatiel's cage is essential to its health and happiness. Since they're so social, the cage will need to be in an area where the bird can engage with the whole family. As pointed out in Chapter 4, cockatiels can suffer distress if left alone too long. At the same time, we know too much stimulation can cause problems. Hence, it's smart not to put the cage in a high-traffic area, yet it needs to be where there is interaction and communication, preferably a family room; one shared by the household works best.

    Cockatiels need to feel safe. Placing the cage in a corner where the two walls form sides will provide that security. Even if this isn't possible, one wall will work and perhaps with a drape on the other side. It's not a good idea to put the cage directly in front of a window. Barking dogs, wild birds, and inclement weather can upset the bird. A partial window view is fine. Like humans, cockatiels need vitamin D. However, windows filter out UV rays, your Cockatiel will need natural sunlight or you can get a UV light to keep the bird healthy, especially in winter months. There are various types of these lights on the market, but before buying and using one, it's wise to talk with your avian vet. That way, you can discuss the setup at home and decide what will work best for you and your cockatiel.
    The cage needs to be out of the direct path of heating and AC vents. Likewise, you wouldn't want it in a bathroom with the constant changes in heat and humidity. The kitchen is also a big NO. Besides the temperature changes, there are the fumes from cooking and self-cleaning ovens, as well as nonstick pans.
    You'll also want to be sure the cage is secure and placed on an even surface. Regarding hanging cages and standing cages, remember the size

CHAPTER 5: Creating a Home

chart from the previous section and choose wisely. It's doubtful you'll find a hanging cage large enough to accommodate your cockatiel's wingspan.

Cage Bedding

The word bedding is a bit of a misnomer because it's not something your cockatiel will sleep in. Birds tend to sleep on a high perch. Rather, bedding here refers to what the bottom of the cage will be lined with and is just one option for you to choose from. There's also paper lining. Opinions on which is best are widely subjective. It may depend on your preference for ease of cleaning, cost, your bird's behavior, or any number of things. Regardless of what you choose, you're going to need something you can clean daily, something your bird won't eat, not scented and/or toxic, with no dust. Let's examine the differences between bedding and paper liners.

Photo Courtesy of Laura Williams

Paper Lining

More often than not, experts suggest paper lining is better than bedding, the main reason being you can easily monitor the bird's droppings for signs of health issues. Your cockatiel's droppings are made up of three elements and should look a certain way. (I'll talk more about healthy poops in Chapter 8.) By having paper for them to go on, you can observe its regularity and consistency. If using bedding, which is usually made of shavings or straw, you won't be able to look so closely.

Paper can be simple to get. You can use packing paper, paper towels, brown paper bags, butcher paper, or newspaper. Newspaper is not toxic, although you might want to stay away from the shiny, colored ads. You can even find it for free! If you live near a newspaper office, you can ask for old papers that are outdated. They also have rolls with pieces left on them that are too small for their use, but that will work perfectly for you. Local libraries may have newspapers they're looking to recycle. Even hospitals and nursing homes are an option. Hotels, coffee shops—use your imagination, and save yourself some cash.

Experiment with where to place the paper. On top of the grate will keep the grate clean. But if your bird chews on the paper, you may need to put it under the grates on the substrate. Either way, it will catch food, water, and droppings and can be changed daily.

Use a spray bottle to mist the paper before removing it from the cage's substrate. This will prevent dander and down feathers from flying in the air. It's an added protection for your lungs.

Bedding

Just because a bag of bedding can be bought in a pet store doesn't mean it's safe. You should avoid bedding made of pine (which can have oils), nutshells, and cat litter because all of these can be scented and dusty, not to mention messy if your bird is flinging them out of the cage. Further, it is difficult to monitor the condition of droppings in these shavings. Some bedding, like straw, will even mold. This is why paper liners are the most recommended.

CHAPTER 5: Creating a Home

Food and Water Bowls

The cage you purchase will probably come with plastic food and water bowls. However, this might not be the best choice for your cockatiel. Plastic is porous, which leaves lots of places for bacteria to hide. Not to mention, your bird may chew on it and make even more cracks and crevices for germs to burrow into. It's just safer and a simpler clean-up to use stainless steel water and food bowls. They're only slightly more expensive but will last a lifetime.

Something to think about is the placement of the food and water bowls. It's best to have them on the sides of the cage with a perch slightly higher than the bowls. If they are in the corners of the cage, your cockatiel may want to use them as perches.

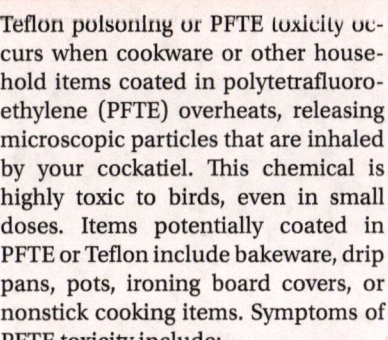

HEALTH ALERT

Teflon Poisoning (PFTE Toxicity)

Teflon poisoning or PFTE toxicity occurs when cookware or other household items coated in polytetrafluoroethylene (PFTE) overheats, releasing microscopic particles that are inhaled by your cockatiel. This chemical is highly toxic to birds, even in small doses. Items potentially coated in PFTE or Teflon include bakeware, drip pans, pots, ironing board covers, or nonstick cooking items. Symptoms of PFTE toxicity include:
- Respiratory distress
- Tail bobbing
- Bird dropping from perch
- Open-mouthed or raspy breathing.

PFTE toxicity is often fatal, and prevention is the best defense against this condition. Removing nonstick cookware or other Teflon-coated items from the home could save your bird's life.

Bath Time

Later, we'll discuss bath time in depth because there are several options. But for now, think about whether you want a bath to be kept in the cage with the bird. There are some adorable options to choose from, but don't forget all the safety measures taken so far. It's simple enough to use a stainless-steel bowl for baths in the same way you do for food and water.

Perches

> *A variety of perch types will be very beneficial to your bird's feet. We recommend an assortment of natural-style wood perches, rope perches, and grooming perches. The grooming perch should be placed lower, while the rope perch should be placed higher. Cockatiels are most likely to sleep on the highest perch, so ensuring that the highest perch is the comfiest is very important. When setting up the cage, you'll also want to include an assortment of toys. Getting toys with different materials and textures is a good way to learn what your new bird likes to play with and is great for enrichment.*
>
> JESSICA OEGEMA
> *Casa la Parrot*

Another reason for having a big enough cage is what you're going to fill it with. Let's start with perches. Your cockatiel will spend a lot of time on its perches, so it's wise to take a cue from the wild. In the wild, cockatiels land on branches of various sizes, shapes, and surfaces. This provides exercise for their feet and can help keep their nails trimmed. Standing on the same perch day in and day out will damage your cockatiel's feet.

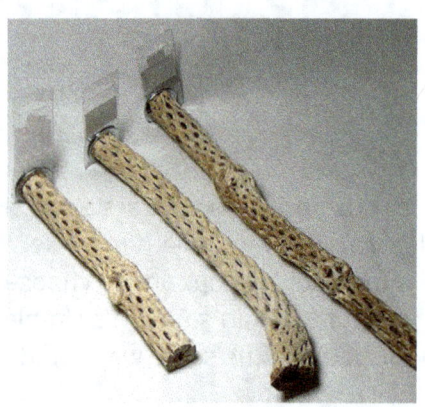

So, when it comes to choosing perches, think about different textures, sizes, and materials. Most breeders and specialists recommend that you not use the perches and dowels that come with the purchase of a new cage. Those dowels are slick and have no variation in size. Using them can lead to bumblefoot, which is a condition we'll talk

CHAPTER 5: Creating a Home

about in Chapter 8. Likewise, don't use sand or sandpaper perches because they can cause irritation on the bottom of the feet. It's best to have two to three types of perches in the cage made from rope, wood, cement, or cholla.

Photo Courtesy of Kim O'Toole

Once you've chosen the perches, find the best places to position them in the cage. They need to be at various levels in the cage to encourage climbing and movement. Don't place them too close to the sides where the bird can hit its tail feathers on the bars, and don't place them directly over food and water bowls. Although the food and water bowls need to be easily accessible, don't put them where they can become contaminated by feces or food falling into the water. Since birds like to be high up most of the time, you'll want the rope perch higher than the other perches. They tend to sleep higher up, and the rope is more comfortable for sleeping.

Toys, Toys, and More Toys

You can never have too many toys for your cockatiel. Not that you want them in the cage all at once, especially in the bird's first month at home. Instead, it's nice to have a rotation of toys as a means of enrichment. These birds are very smart and love to keep busy. They have the intelligence of a three-year-old, so giving them something to concentrate on is great for their mental health.

Here are some examples of toys they love.

- Chew toys
- Preening toys
- Foraging toys
- Perch toys
- Edible toys

As with everything we've said so far, safety is key when it comes to picking out toys for your cockatiel. Always research the product you're buying for your feathered friend. It's not wise to buy or accept second-hand toys as gifts. It's too easy for germs to be passed to your bird. Cockatiels love toys made with brightly colored palm leaves, especially something with tassels. They'll use these for shredding and preening. Little piñata style toys are fun as well. Your bird can pull out the tiny bits for hours.

Cockatiels enjoy ladders and love rattan balls. Swinging perches are favorites because it feels like sitting on a branch in the wild. The movement comes naturally to them. Then, there are more permanent toys and perches you can use outside of the cage, like bird gyms and playgrounds. These come in handy when you're cleaning the cage. It gives your bird something to focus on while you're in its personal space, spritzing and wiping. Puzzle toys are another great way to keep your bird distracted while you clean the cage, and it's fun to watch your bird solve them!

If you're into DIY projects or simply want to save money, there are tons of treats and toys you can make for your bird. For instance, remember the Chinese finger traps you used to get at birthday parties? Well, those can be turned into enrichment toys. Just shove a snack inside, maybe a few bits of shredded paper, and let your bird have fun with it. Another simple enrichment is to take a small, sturdy glass bowl, place some millet seed in it, and then throw some shredded paper in it so that the bird has to forage for the seed. Then there's always the ever-present empty toilet paper roll. Pop some of your bird's favorite snack inside, stuff some shredded paper in, and then let the bird have at it. One thing to remember when using shredded paper like this is to be sure it's colored with food dye so it won't harm your cockatiel. You can find this at pet stores. More than anything, keep your bird entertained. Mix things up a bit. If you use a finger trap with a hidden snack in one corner of the cage, move it to a different area next time.

Finally, to mirror or not to mirror? Mirrors are a sticky subject among bird experts. Some see no harm in birds having a companion in the mirror and believe it will not stop them from bonding with their owner. Others think it will cause the bird to try to bond with the image in the mirror. So, this is a toy you will have to make your own decision about. And, of course,

CHAPTER 5: Creating a Home

it's something you can discuss with your avian vet. As for my family, we chose not to have a mirror with Shelly (formerly Sheldon) because she'd already had a previous owner, and we didn't want to take a chance on anything preventing her from becoming comfortable with us.

FUN FACT
Cholla Wood

Pronounced "choya," cholla wood isn't actually wood. It doesn't come from trees but from dried out cacti.

Warnings

I cannot stress safety enough. Research a product before buying it. Are the materials safe for cockatiels? Is it made by a reputable bird toy manufacturer? Go beyond reviews that say, "My bird loves it," to find out what the product is made of. For instance, as a cockatiel owner, I recommended wooden perches. Yet, there are types of wood toxic to birds, such as cherry, cedar, and any treated wood. The same thing goes for rope. You want to use a rope perch in your cage, but it needs to be made of all-natural fibers like cotton or hemp. Never use one made of nylon, as it can hurt your bird. What about toys with bells? The clapper inside could be made of lead. Err on the side of caution if you want a shiny bell or toy that clangs and look for stainless steel. I think you can see why it's important to do your homework when buying bird toys.

Most of all, be observant. Because, like a child who can have an accident playing with its toys, your bird can still get injured playing with "bird-safe" toys. As I've said from Chapter 1 on, owning a cockatiel is a years-long commitment. You will never stop being responsible for its safety and well-being.

CHAPTER 6

Dietary Needs

Pellets and Seeds

It may be tempting to feed your cockatiel a special treat as soon as you bring it home. After all, you want to begin bonding right away, and food can and will be a part of that experience. Remember, though, that you're going to be giving your bird time and space to adjust to its new surroundings. By following the diet it has already been on, you'll be able to maintain some normalcy for the bird. Give the bird a couple of weeks, maybe even a month, before introducing new foods.

Food	Percentage of Daily Diet
Seeds	10%
Pellets	70%
Fruits	5%
Greens	5%
Vegetables	10%

Balance

Be sure you know what your bird was raised on and discuss transitioning the bird to a different diet with the breeder or your avian vet. Because when you are ready to expand your cockatiel's culinary palate, balance is key. Birds can be picky eaters. They may favor one seed over another, which can lead to a lack of nutrition. For example, they love millet and sunflower seeds and may actually eat only those two from a blend of seeds. And though seeds are fine, an all-seed diet may be lacking in calcium and vitamin A. So, seeds should be only a small part of your cockatiel's diet, around 10%. One and a half to two tablespoons of seeds a day is plenty. If you find at the end of the day there are seeds left over in the bowl, you can cut back on the amount given each day.

> *You want to minimize the amount of stress your new bird may experience as he may be overwhelmed and scared; he may be unsure of himself and refuse to eat or drink. You should follow the same routine and diet he was weaned on or was eating until he settles in. Babies may cry and bob their heads if they are not weaned, although crying can last several months. Newly weaned birds can regress and starve themselves to death by just playing with their food and not eating it. Look for poop to confirm he is eating. If the bird is not eating and drinking after 48 hours, you MUST contact the breeder or a vet immediately. Do not make any changes to his diet other than offering new items such as healthy sprouts, veggies, or chop.*
>
> BRIDGET MARQUEZ
> *Marquez Tiels*

Pellets are a great source of nutrition for your cockatiel. They've been designed to meet a variety of your bird's dietary needs. Pellets will come in different shapes, sizes, and colors, but don't forget about what was said concerning the colored paper. The same is true for pellets. Only natural food dyes are the best. You can find pellets specifically for your bird's size, so be aware of whether you're getting pellets that are too large. Pellets will make up about 70% of your bird's diet. You want to keep the bowl three-quarters full and refresh it daily.

Fruits and vegetables combined will make up the remaining 20% of your bird's meal plan. The next section will go into detail about which fruits and veggies to use and which ones to avoid.

Boutin's Journal

My granddaughter feeds her cockatiels Kaytee Rainbow Cockatiel Food. The pellets are in different shapes and sizes, but her picky little Polly won't eat the red pieces that are shaped like half-moons. She culls out everything else and leaves those behind.

Recommended Brands

Roudybush Daily Maintenance Bird Food: Contains no added sugars or colors and uses all-natural preservatives

Harrison's Bird Foods High Potency Fine: No preservatives, artificial colors, sweeteners for flavors, certified organic, and Non-GMO verified

CHAPTER 6: Dietary Needs

LAFEBER'S Premium Daily Diet Pellets Pet Bird Food: No preservatives, artificial colors, sweeteners for flavors, certified organic, and Non-GMO verified

Kaytee Exact Rainbow Premium Daily Nutrition for Cockatiels: Omega 3s, prebiotics and probiotics, naturally preserved

Fruits, Veggles, and Greens

> *Variety is key! The more foods you can get them to accept, the better. You wouldn't want to eat the same things day in and day out, and neither will your bird. I feed mine lots of mixed veggies, quinoa, couscous, and dark, leafy greens. Fruits aren't as important as they have a lot of sugar. But anything you're eating that's good for you is good for your bird!*
>
> LISA SZUMITA
> *Utah Parrots*

Variety is the spice of life is a line from a poem written in 1785, yet it still holds true. We all like a little variety in everything we do, but especially in what we eat. Your cockatiel is no different. So, let's look at some ways to keep food time, fun time.

I'll start with what not to feed cockatiels, beginning with canned fruits and vegetables. Although there's nothing inherently wrong with canned fruits and vegetables, they're going to have very little

Photo Courtesy of Cozzi Larsen

nutritional value. Fruits may have added sugars and preservatives, while vegetables will have added sodium. Fresh is the way to go.

Safe Fruits and Vegetables

You can leave the peels on washed fruits, but make sure any seeds are removed.

Cockatiels can also eat fresh herbs like basil, cilantro, dandelion, ginger root, oregano, rosemary, and dry cinnamon. Avoid nutmeg, though, as it is toxic for cockatiels. These fruits and vegetables will make up about 20% of your bird's diet, but less is best when it comes to fruits. Fruit should be used sparingly as a training tool. Since fruits are high in sugar, too much can be dangerous for your cockatiel's health. A cockatiel should not be eating fruit every day. At most, only three or four times a week. Always, always wash fresh fruits and vegetables before serving. They're more than likely to have been sprayed with pesticides. Some people use soap and water mixture, while others simply use water. Personally, I do this with the fruit and veggies my whole family eats: I use three parts water to one part vinegar to soak them in. After 15 minutes, I rinse and re-rinse them before letting them dry.

Even when you've washed the fruits and vegetables, take the time to inspect them before serving. Mushy or rotten spots can cause mold, which is toxic for the

Photo Courtesy of Jennifer White

CHAPTER 6: Dietary Needs

Safe Fruits and Vegetables

- Dark leafy greens (every other day)
- Peas
- Grains
- Sprouts
- Beans
- Peppers (red, green, hot)
- Broccoli
- Bananas
- Cherries (no pits)
- Peaches
- Blueberries
- Grapes
- Mango
- Melons
- Zucchini
- Cabbage
- Apples
- Cucumbers
- Pomegranate
- Kiwi

bird. Be sure to remove any uneaten fruits or vegetables within 12 hours so they don't spoil.

Read what **Colleen L. Rivas at The Purple Parrot LLC** says about feeding fresh fruit to cockatiels.

> *In nature, parrots eat fruits when they are unripened. They do this in order to eat the fruit before other animals. When we give cockatiels fruit from the grocery stores, they are usually ripe and at their max level of sugar. People tend to feed their cockatiels those fruits, thinking they are doing a good thing. Excessive sweets are not a good thing, as it leads to liver issues with parrots.*

While most vegetables are better given raw, cockatiels prefer cooked pumpkin and sweet potatoes.

Cuttlebone

Cuttlefish Bone

Technically, cuttlebone doesn't fall into any of the food categories we've gone over, but it's an important part of your bird's diet. Cuttlebone isn't actually a bone. It comes from the cuttlefish and is a type of internal shell. It's rich in calcium and other minerals a cockatiel needs. It helps with digestion, as well as bone and feather strength. It's inexpensive, and you can clip it to the side of the cage for easy access. If your bird is reluctant to eat it, you can shave off bits of the cuttlebone and sprinkle it across the food.

Stubborn Eaters

If your cockatiel was raised on an all-seed and pellet diet, there's a good chance it doesn't even know that vegetables are food. It will be up to you to teach him. However, simply plopping a piece of broccoli in the bowl might not work. So, here are a couple of tips and tricks you can use to generate your cockatiel's interest in vegetables. Bear in mind what I said about cockatiels having the intellect of a three-year-old—they can have some of the same finicky opinions about veggies as three-year-olds do. Still, with some patience, you can turn your little friend into a veggie lover.

Something you can try from the outset is different shapes, sizes, and textures. I don't mean cut the zucchini into cute little teddy bears, but try julienne or cube cuts; even smash it with a fork. You can be sneaky and toss some small, chopped veggies in a bowl and then sprinkle some of the bird's beloved seeds on top. As the bird forages through the vegetables for the seed, he will manage to get a piece or two of the vegetables as well. You can get creative and take a bell pepper (keep its seeds, but toss any stem parts) and cut the bottom half off so that it forms a small bowl. Place some of the seeds in the bottom sections of the pepper and let the bird try it out. This can be done with other vegetables as well, like a thick broccoli stalk or the inside of a cucumber. Anything, really. This will give the bird the taste of the vegetable and build a palate for it.

> **HELPFUL TIP**
> **How Much is Enough?**
>
> The easiest way to know if your cockatiel is getting enough to eat is by examining its weight and droppings. Adult cockatiels weigh between 70 and 125 grams, with females tending toward the lower end of the range and males toward the upper. If your bird produces too few or unusually watery droppings, it may not be getting enough to eat. Cockatiels can also be prone to obesity if their diet is too high in fat. Consult with your veterinarian if you're concerned about your cockatiel's eating habits, and be sure to offer an array of fresh food for each meal.

Another thing you can do is play a little reverse psychology on your bird. Allow it to sit beside you or on your shoulder while you have a vegetable snack. Like children, the more a cockatiel thinks it can't have something, the more it wants it. I'm not saying be a tease, but allow the bird to be curious about what you're eating. Maybe say no once, turn away, and then allow the bird to test-taste.

You can also blend up a smoothie. Just puree a few vegetables and let the bird have a try. Or take a leaf of bok choy, kale, or any leafy green and weave it through the bars of the cage. Birds will naturally pick at it, and if you wash it before hanging it, they'll bathe in the water dripping from it. There are all kinds of foraging toys you can use for offering your bird its vegetables. Skewers are great for loading different pieces of varying colors and textures. Hang them in the cage and allow the bird to help itself.

Finally, the best time to introduce a new vegetable to your cockatiel is in the morning when it is hungry. And I would advise against using fruit as an incentive, mixing it with vegetables to tempt the bird. If it develops a taste for the fruit first, it might be harder to get them to eat the vegetables. Save fruit for treat time.

> *Seeds are like the chocolate cake of the parrot world. But even though seeds taste amazing to the birds, they should not be in a cockatiel's daily diet. Pellets and chop should be the daily diet plan, with seeds being offered as a special treat once a week.*
>
> COLLEEN L. RIVAS
> *The Purple Parrot*

CHAPTER 6: Dietary Needs

Chop

You may have heard the word chop when looking into what to feed your cockatiel. Chop is exactly what it says it is, a finely chopped blend of vegetables to feed your bird. You can use a food processor or chop it by hand. Be careful that it's not mashed and squishy. Small chunks will allow for the bird to pick through it. In the beginning, you can use a food the bird already likes and mix it in. This will encourage him to eat the  chop. Use about one-third of his regular food and stir it into the chop right before serving. Chop can be frozen and then thawed daily. That said, your bird may prefer it fresh, as the texture of frozen vegetables changes. If that's the case, keep your chop in an airtight container in the refrigerator. Over time, you can experiment with different ingredients, even adding in cooked grains and legumes like quinoa, barley, lentils, and chickpeas (cooked according to directions).

Sample Chop Blend

- ✓ 3 green vegetables
- ✓ 3 of a red/yellow/orange/purple vegetable
- ✓ 1 herb/spice/edible flower.

Tip: Fruit makes chop watery.

Treats

First, let me clarify what I mean by treats. I'm not talking about the slice of red pepper you put in one of your DIY enrichment toys as a snack. The treats I'm speaking of here are truly something sweet or a little on the indulgent side. They're not intended to be sustenance or a substitute for a good diet. These goodies should be given sparingly, maybe once a month. You don't want your cockatiel to give up the nutritious foods that are keeping him healthy because he'd rather eat treats. Here are some ideas for that special once-a-month treat.

- Cheerios
- Honey Stick
- Millet Spray
- Dried Mealworms
- Natural Low-Iron Baby Foods

Never Feed Your Bird These

- Avocado
- Chocolate
- Caffeine
- Alcohol
- Iceberg lettuce (mostly liquid with little nutrition)
- Onions
- Garlic
- Tomatoes
- Sweeteners (natural or otherwise)
- Salt
- Seeds from fruits (apples, pears, oranges, etc.)
- Fruit pits
- Rhubarb
- Tea
- Houseplants
- Sugar-free candy
- Any high-fat/ high-sodium/ high-sugar foods

Water

This should seem obvious, but fresh water is essential. Food and water bowls should be washed with soap and water daily. Think about it: would you want to eat and drink out of the same dirty dishes day in and day out? Not only is it unappealing, but it's also a hazard. Bacteria can build up from rotting food. Feces could have inadvertently been spread to the bowls. So, wash them daily.

If you use well water in your home, it's best to buy distilled water for your pet. Personally, I use a Britta and drink filtered water, and so does Shelly. They don't require much because they're adapted to living in the drier climates of Australia and naturally don't drink a lot. So, it's not that big of an added cost, especially for the peace of mind.

CHAPTER 7
Basic Care

> *Enrichment through hanging foods from the sides or top of the cage for your bird to 'forage' is an important, healthy activity for a cockatiel to engage in; it nurtures their natural instinct to 'hunt' for food. You can hide nuts or seeds in premade foraging toys, but it can also be fun to make your own. Simply fill a box with whatever foods or nuts you've chosen and let your bird root through it to find the goodies. This activity is entertaining for your cockatiel, and good for its mental health as well!*
>
> COLLEEN L. RIVAS
> *The Purple Parrot*

Photo Courtesy of Robin Koczwara

This chapter gets to the heart of why we say having a cockatiel requires commitment. We'll look at cleaning the cage, grooming and bathing, household dangers to watch for, preferences about covering the cage at night, and whether to trim flight feathers. It's not my intention to offend anyone when I compare some of the care of a cockatiel to that of a child, but the truth is, unlike diapers that children eventually grow out of, cleaning a cage is never-ending. It

CHAPTER 7: Basic Care

will be what you do for the entirety of the bird's life. So, let me repeat myself and say: getting a cockatiel should not be an impulse purchase.

Now, if I haven't frightened you away, let's talk about cleaning your friend's home.

Cleaning the Cage

> *Your bird's food and water must be changed daily, and the dishes should be washed with soap. The cage should be cleaned weekly, including the bottom tray, grate, perches, and toys. Also make sure to check the toys frequently to ensure they are still safe. Ratty rope can become a hazard, as can many other things ... but checking them daily can prevent injuries or even death.*
>
> JESSICA OEGEMA
> *Casa la Parrot*

There are two types of cleaning when it comes to your cockatiel's cage: once-a-day spot cleaning and once-a-week deep cleaning.

Daily

Before doing any cleaning, make sure your cockatiel is in a safe place, protected from dust or dander that might float into the air. Cockatiels have delicate respiratory systems, so breathing in dust and dander during daily cleanings can be harmful. Additionally, protect your own respiratory system by wearing a face mask. Water and food bowls (and the bath, if it is inside the cage) should be washed with soap and water daily. Remember, fresh fruits and vegetables should not be left in the cage for more than 12 hours. Paper linings need to be replaced every day, twice a day if you have more than one cockatiel. Misting the paper lining with a disinfectant spray before removing it will help keep some of that dander from flying around.

Photo Courtesy of Timea Kovacs

Products You'll Need
Antibacterial spray
Wire brush
Dustpan and brush
Paper towels and/or rags
Face masks
Paper lining or bedding

For the bars, perches, and toys, simply dampen paper towels or a rag with the same disinfectant and wipe off discarded food and bird droppings. A great DIY cleaning solution can be made with a mix of 50% water and 50% distilled vinegar. There are other products out there for disinfecting the cage, but vinegar is safe and doesn't have to be rinsed off since it won't harm your bird.

Weekly

Once a week, the cage will need a deep cleaning. Start by removing toys, perches, and food and water bowls. Toys and perches need a good deep cleaning as well. This is also a good time to inspect them for damage and replace or discard broken components. Make sure there's no food or feces in hidden places on toys and perches where the bird could inadvertently eat something contaminated. Your DIY vinegar solution works especially well for this. You won't have to worry about your bird ingesting a toxic cleaner.

HELPFUL TIP
Beaking vs. Biting

Cockatiels often use their beaks like humans use their hands—to stabilize or climb. Additionally, cockatiels have many nerve endings in their tongues, which they use to evaluate new textures and flavors. This exploratory behavior is called "beaking" and, while not always gentle, is much softer than a cockatiel bite. While cockatiels are relatively docile birds, they may be provoked into biting in self-defense or out of fear.

Using a wire brush, scrape off dried droppings from the cage bars and ledges and let them fall to the paper liner you'll remove later. This step will save muscle power when it's time to wipe the bars. With the surface droppings removed, spray the bars with the disinfectant. Be sure to spray the solution into cracks and crevices. Paper towels are great for wiping the bars clean. However, if you prefer to use rags and a bucket of water, make sure your cockatiel doesn't get into the bucket of water. Birds can drown easily.

Once you've removed the dampened paper liner, it's time to clean the substrate and/or grate in the bottom of the cage. Depending on your home, the two pieces can be taken outside to be sprayed with the cleaning solution and then hosed off with water. Or it's just as easy to do it in a bathtub using a cup or pitcher to rinse them.

Finally, use the dustpan and brush to sweep up any debris on the floor and furnishings around the outside of the cage. Before returning your cockatiel to its home, make sure everything is dry—cage, toys, and

Photo Courtesy of Joan Indursky

perches. This is also a great time to provide your bird with some enrichment. Instead of placing everything in the same location it was, move things around. Change up ladder placement. Swap out toys for different ones. Put a perch on the opposite side from its previous position. Your bird will appreciate the clean cage and the new challenges.

Grooming

> *Checking nail growth is important on a monthly basis. I use a small nail cutter, or even better yet, a nail grinder—just a regular one that is used for cats or dogs will do just fine. If you do not feel comfortable trimming your bird's nails, an avian vet will be able to perform this procedure at a very low cost. If you bought your cockatiel from a breeder, they may offer a nail- and wing-clipping service free of charge—it's a good question to ask your breeder when inquiring about a cockatiel.*
>
> **COLLEEN L. RIVAS**
> *The Purple Parrot*

Cockatiels are relatively low maintenance when it comes to grooming. You'll want to keep an eye on your cockatiel's beak, nails, and flight feathers, which we'll discuss more later in this chapter. The beak usually doesn't require anything from you. Daily use—preening, eating, climbing, using it like a tool—keeps the beak healthy. You may notice the beak peeling, but this is normal. Cockatiels' beaks are made of the same thing our fingernails are made of, and since they use them on different surfaces and textures, beaks will peel just like a fingernail. But if you notice your bird has abnormal beak growth, it's crooked, or generally looking poorly, take the bird to the vet, as this may be a sign of an underlying condition. You never want to trim your bird's beak yourself because you could hurt the bird.

Your avian vet is also your go-to for nail trimming. Trimming doesn't have to be done often, just every few weeks to months. It's not recommended that you trim your bird's nails yourself because it's too easy to injure the bird.

Baths

> *Giving your birds a bath occasionally is good enrichment. They may like being misted, placed in the sink with slow-running water, having a big bowl in their cage, or even taking a shower with you!"*
>
> JESSICA OEGEMA
> *Casa la Parrot*

Regular bathing will maintain the health of your cockatiel's skin and feathers. An unkempt bird may become irritable, pluck feathers, or bite at the skin. Cockatiels in the wild bathe frequently to control their dust and dander, so offer your bird a bath every day. It may not take one that often, but give it the opportunity.

There are several techniques you can use for training your bird to bathe. The first is to use a spray bottle for a gentle shower. Water should be at room temperature and sprayed in a light mist. Don't spray the water directly at your bird. Try spraying in the air near the bird and allow it to come to the water. Make sure the bottle is cleaned frequently to prevent mold and grime build-up. This type of bathing can be a bonding experience for you and your bird.

Photo Courtesy of Cozzi Larsen

Once you've introduced baths to your cockatiel, bathing under the kitchen or bathroom tap is a fun option. Run the water on low. Like the spray bottle, the water should be at room temperature. You can provide a shallow bowl in the sink for the bird to splash around in.

Some people shower with their birds. In our home, we don't, but it is certainly an alternative. If you choose the shower, don't place your cockatiel directly under the showerhead. The water pressure could harm it. Like with the spray bottle or sink, allow the bird to venture into the water on their own.

Introduce one of these forms of bathing to your bird and give the bird time to adapt. If the bird appears hesitant, vary the ways offered, as well as the time of day. Your bird may not be a morning bather. You don't have to force your cockatiel to take a bath. They generally love bathing. Simply be patient and allow your bird time to decide which form it likes best. It will learn to bathe and enjoy it on its own.

When the bird has bathed, allow the bird to air dry. Birds dry off naturally in the wild. Just make sure the room isn't cold, the bird isn't in the direct path of a draft, and let the bird air dry. Never use a blow drier to dry your bird.

Lastly, don't use any shampoos or manufactured products on your cockatiel. They're not necessary. If your bird has access to a bath of fresh water, the bird will be fine.

Daily	Weekly	Monthly
Spot clean cage	Deep clean cage	
Check the condition of nails and beak	Inspect feather health	Have nails trimmed
Offer bath		

CHAPTER 7: Basic Care

Covering the Cage at Night

Photo Courtesy of Kennadi Manning

There are varying opinions on whether a bird's cage should be covered. Some birds will sleep better in complete darkness when the cage is covered, while others may have night frights, and the cover only makes it worse. We'll talk more about night frights in Chapter 9, but ultimately, be patient and allow your cockatiel to express its preference when it comes to covering its cage.

Trimming Flight Feathers

> *Keeping wings trimmed, though a personal choice, can prevent your bird from flying away if it ever gets outside. If a bird escapes, it is very likely that it will not come back. Trimmed wings can also make handling and training your bird easier—if it can't get away when it wants, it will rely more on you. If your bird's wings are trimmed, you can let it out to wander around—just make sure it is always supervised. Like a young child, birds can get into things that are harmful to them very quickly!*
>
> **JESSICA OEGEMA**
> *Casa la Parrot*

Photo Courtesy of Mary Kelly

CHAPTER 7: Basic Care

Trimming feathers is a somewhat controversial topic, so much so that it's impossible to make a pros and cons list on the subject. For instance, some specialists say trimming wings keeps the bird safe by preventing it from flying out of a window. Other specialists will say this isn't true. The bird can and will still fly, and clipping its wings can cause it to have balance problems, which creates a greater danger for the bird. If you're worried about the bird flying away, don't let him out of the cage until you've had time to train him to learn to step up and follow your commands. As with a dog's safety, you want to be able to call your bird to you and have it obey.

HEALTH ALERT
Cockatiel Dander

Cockatiels produce a fine, powdery substance known as dander. While this is normal and harmless to most, it can cause issues for individuals with respiratory conditions or allergies. If you have asthma, allergies, or other respiratory concerns, it's essential to monitor how cockatiel dander affects you. Regular cleaning, using air purifiers, and ensuring proper ventilation can help manage dander levels and minimize potential irritation. Always consult with a healthcare provider to ensure that having a cockatiel is safe for your specific health needs.

If you are unsure about clipping or not clipping, have a discussion with your avian vet. Bear in mind, though, that clipping wings is not the same as cutting your hair. This is a part of a bird's movement. A bird has to work twice as hard to fly with less wingspan. Whatever you do, don't try to clip the wings yourself. Leave it to a trained professional because feathers are a large part of a bird's overall health. One last thing—remember, flying is your bird's first line of defense, so really weigh it out before making your decision.

CHAPTER 8

Health and Illness

Proper Planning

> *Seek out a good avian vet BEFORE bringing your new bird home! Be certain that your vet is a true avian vet and doesn't just say, 'Oh yeah, we can see your bird.' Birds are nothing like dogs and cats. They are delicate, so they can become injured much more easily than a dog or a cat can, and they are masters at hiding illness. They need a veterinarian who has actually been trained in avian medicine.*
>
> DANA GRIMM
> *Beaks and Tweets Aviary*

When it comes to your cockatiel's health, be proactive. Don't wait until your bird is sick before having a plan of action in place. This is something you can start on before you ever purchase your bird. Just because a vet says he'll treat your cockatiel doesn't mean it's a good idea to have him do so. Birds aren't common pets. So, if a vet normally treats cats and dogs, they may not know what is needed for caring for your cockatiel.

An avian vet specializes in birds. Research possible vets. There are plenty of resources online, including Facebook groups and YouTube channels. Ask questions about neighborhood vets and read reviews. A little homework can go a long way toward easing your mind. Once again, cockatiels can live for nearly two decades, so your pet is going to need

CHAPTER 8: Health and Illness

regular check-ups and care. It's a good idea to find a vet that will be with you for the life of the bird. They can also be a resource for you in those first days and weeks when you bring your sweet friend home.

You can also help your vet with the care of your cockatiel by being prepared with a health history of your bird. If possible, family and breeding records from the breeder would be beneficial. Maybe a rundown of the bird's health, diet, and any other information the breeder could share. Anything you can do to assist your avian vet will make it more possible for you to have a happy, healthy cockatiel.

Finally, ask what and how your vet responds to emergencies. Find out how to contact them and/or where to go in case of an emergency. Enter that phone number into your contacts!

Be Vigilant

You are your cockatiel's primary source for health and safety. Vigilance is important. I speak from experience. My daughter's first bird was a parakeet, and one day while cleaning the house, I opened a window to air out the room without even thinking about the bird. The little thing flew away, and my daughter was devastated. I felt like a horrible mother, a horrible human being. It was a split-second decision that caused us all heartache.

Aside from a mishap like this, simply being aware of your bird's routines and mannerisms can help keep it safe and protected. So, stay aware of your bird.

Signs of a Healthy Cockatiel

Part of staying vigilant is knowing what to look for in your bird's demeanor and daily routine. Cockatiels are active birds. They're always on the hunt for something to do. If you notice yours is being unsocial, not wanting to play with its toys, or not eating well, these might be warning flags. Your cockatiel should be sleeping at night and awake in the daytime. Keep an eye on the food bowl to make sure the bird is eating regularly. When you first bring the bird home, it's normal for it to go a day without eating. Beyond that, they should be eating well.

The cockatiel should also be pooping anywhere from 18 to 26+ times a day. (This is why the paper lining needs to be changed daily.) To clarify, the droppings are more than feces. Droppings are composed of urine, feces, and urates. The urine should be clear, while feces will be in solid tube shapes in the center of the droppings. Urates are uric acid

HELPFUL TIP

Pet Insurance or Health Savings?

Pet insurance is health insurance for your pets. Depending on your insurance plan, coverage, monthly payments, and deductibles will vary. Some pet insurance agencies offer exotic pet insurance plans that cover cockatiels, but these exotic or avian pet plans may be challenging to acquire. An alternative to pet insurance is a designated savings account for your cockatiel's health needs. You'll want to deposit a lump sum in this account when you bring your cockatiel home and then decide on a set monthly amount you'll transfer to this account. Setting aside money for unexpected or annual vet bills can help ease some of the stress of bird ownership.

crystals that appear chalky white in the droppings and should never be solid or liquid, but rather something in between. If the cockatiel is not going frequently, or if the bird has diarrhea or becomes constipated, there is a problem. Besides what the droppings look like, their place in the cage can be an indication something is wrong as well. If the day's droppings are nearly all in one spot, it means the bird hasn't been moving about, which is a definite sign of trouble.

Photo Courtesy of Vivi Victorino

Your cockatiel's eyes should not be red, runny, or swollen. Rather, they should be alert, bright, and clear. The same goes for the nares, which are the cockatiel's nostrils. Healthy nostrils are dry, and the feathers around them should be clean.

Feet health is important since your cockatiel spends most of its time on its feet. We talked about perches and how different types and sizes are good for the bird's feet. Without exercise, feet can become arthritic. They can also develop a condition called bumblefoot. Bumblefoot (pododermatitis) is caused by injury to the bird's foot. Things like improper perch size, perches all the same size, or perches that are too rough can cause irritation that leads to inflammation. Spoiled food and/or feces caked on perches can cause infection in the inflamed skin. Your cockatiel's feet should be pinkish in color and the skin supple. If there is swelling, redness, scabs, a reluctance to walk, or ulcers on the soles of the feet, your bird needs to be seen by the vet right away. If left untreated, bumblefoot can become systemic and lead to your bird's death.

The bird's vent should be clean and dry. The vent is the cloaca, an opening for the bird's digestive, urinary, and reproductive system. It's used to expel droppings and lay eggs. Symptoms to watch for indicating a prolapsed cloaca are a lack of droppings, poor appetite, lethargy, straining, and a fluffed-up appearance.

Healthy feathers should be smooth and not puffed up. If your bird is bathing regularly, there will be little dust, and the feathers will be soft and vibrant. Your bird especially needs vitamin A to grow healthy feathers, so its diet is extremely important.

Red Flags

> *Negative behaviors that develop over time are often caused by hidden environmental factors. Cockatiels, like all parrots, have very sensitive respiratory systems, so cleaning agents, candles, wax melts, nonstick cook pans, and owners who smoke can all have negative affects on their health and mental fitness.*
>
> COLLEEN L. RIVAS
> *The Purple Parrot*

> *Fluffy birds that are inactive or hesitant to play are warning signs you should be alert to. A number of things can be the issue when seeing this—none of them good. Watch for discharge in the nostrils or panting, which can indicate respiratory issues. Closed or sunken-in eyes can also be a sign that your cockatiel is suffering from dehydration.*
>
> SAL SALAFIA, CERTIFIED AVIAN SPECIALIST
> *Exotic Pet Birds, Inc.*

CHAPTER 8: Health and Illness

In addition to these signs and symptoms, watch for the following in your bird:

- Fluffed, plucked, or soiled feathers
- Sitting on the cage floor for extended periods of time
- Wheezing, sneezing, or coughing
- Open-mouthed or labored breathing and/or tail bobbing
- Regurgitation or vomiting
- Runny, bloody, or discolored stools or no stool production
- Straining to pass droppings
- Favoring one foot when not sleeping
- Eye or nasal discharge
- Red or swollen eyes
- Persistently closed eyes or sleeping during the day
- Crusty skin around face and feet
- Loss of appetite

Jessica Oegema of Casa la Parrot gives this advice for monitoring your cockatiel's health:

> *"If your bird is staying puffed up for extended periods of time, has cold toes, a runny nose, sneezes often (a dozen or more times a day), has smelly poops, or is sitting on the bottom of the cage and acting lethargic, it needs to go to the vet immediately. A symptomatic bird is an emergent bird. Finding an avian-certified vet before getting your new bird is a good idea as they can be hard to find in some areas."*

Common Cockatiel Health Issues

Keeping your bird healthy is an ongoing promise you make when you buy it. Birds tend to hide their illnesses, a skill learned in the wild to protect themselves from predators. So it's up to us as their care providers to be attentive and dedicated to giving them our best. We've looked

at some symptoms to watch for in your cockatiel. Here are some of the possible underlying conditions behind these symptoms.

- **Avian chlamydiosis:** This disease is caused by bacteria called chlamydia psittaci. Some refer to it as parrot fever, and it's common in cockatiels. It can cause chronic infections and death. Chlamydiosis can be spread to humans, but it's not connected to the venereal form of chlamydophila in people. Symptoms of avian chlamydiosis include lethargy, a loss of appetite and/or weight, shaking and shivering, breathing problems, nasal discharge, and wet droppings. If you suspect your bird has avian chlamydiosis, take it to the vet for testing. Since the disease is complicated, treatment takes time. The bird will need to be on antibiotics for 45 days. Avian chlamydiosis can be passed to humans by inhaling fecal matter or dust. (Wear that mask when cleaning the cage!) In a human, symptoms are like those of the flu. See your doctor if you suspect you've been infected. Unfortunately, some birds can carry the disease but be asymptomatic and end up spreading it to other birds and humans.

- **Conjunctivitis:** Cockatiels can contract eye infections just like humans. It's not always possible to know what causes it, but knowing what to watch for can help you help your bird sooner rather than later. Here are some signs: watery, swollen, or crusty eyes; sneezing; swelling of the face; and cloudy eyes. A vet will prescribe topical and oral antibiotics for your bird, as well as a saline wash for any physical discomfort.

- **Diarrhea:** A cockatiel's delicate digestive system can be easily upset. Stress or a change in diet can cause diarrhea. It can also be a sign of a more dangerous condition. If your cockatiel has diarrhea for more than 24 hours, contact your vet.

- **Egg binding:** This is a common disorder in female cockatiels. A female does not have to encounter a male to lay an egg. Egg binding happens when the cockatiel is unable to lay the egg, and it becomes stuck in the vent. It can be caused by a poor diet, which leads to a lack of calcium. Issues with the bird's reproductive system can also instigate egg binding. You may even see part of the egg in the opening. Beyond that, here are some symptoms of egg binding: labored breathing, puffed-up feathers, swelling, straining, loss of appetite, sitting on the cage floor, and constipation. Take your bird to the vet immediately for them to assess it and determine the right treatment. This condition can be deadly for the cockatiel, so don't hesitate.

- **Psittacine Beak and Feather Disease, BPFD:** Beak and feather disease is caused by a virus. Birds can become infected through the mouth, the nasal passages, or their vent. Although the virus doesn't affect humans, it is contagious to other birds and is spread through the infected bird's feather dust. It can take months or even years for symptoms (dead or abnormal feathers) to present, and once they do, birds can die within six to 12 months. There is no treatment for the disease, and sadly, it's usually fatal. Continuing to care for your

Photo Courtesy of Jen Thomas

bird by giving it a stress-free environment can help prolong its life. However, an infected bird should be isolated from other birds in the home because the disease is transmittable.

- **Dehydration:** Birds can become dehydrated for many reasons. If discarded food, feathers, dander, and droppings get in the water, the bird may not want to drink out of it. If your bird is on a medication, and you're putting it in the water, the bird may refuse to drink it if it tastes different. Talk to your vet about the best ways to administer medications. Also, make sure the bird knows where the water is. If you've just brought the bird home, maybe jiggle the bottle or water bowl to let the bird know where it is. Some birds prefer drinking from a bottle to drinking from a bowl. If you've done all these things and your bird still isn't drinking, contact the vet. Signs of dehydration include sunken and dull eyes, wrinkles around the eyes, mucous membranes in the mouth that are dry or sticky, reduced skin elasticity, lethargy, weakness, dry droppings, or no droppings.

CHAPTER 9

Emotional Health

How to Bond with Your Cockatiel

> *Learn to read your bird's body language. They will always tell you what you need to know—you just need to learn how to understand it, so hang out with your bird as much as you can. If you miss a day or two of handling, make it up to your pet. They have feelings, and the intelligence of a three-year-old, so it's best not to forget it!*
>
> JESSICA OEGEMA
> *Casa la Parrot*

    The first two weeks after bringing your cockatiel home are the most important and will set the tone for the bird's emotional health. No doubt, you've watched videos of cockatiels doing all sorts of cute things, and you want that experience with your bird, but patience is key in the beginning. Take things slowly, and give your cockatiel time to become comfortable in its new home. It may take anywhere from a few days to a couple of weeks for the bird to get comfortable, and you'll need to limit your interactions during that time. Don't rush the process. When you're satisfied the bird is eating and sleeping well and maybe exhibiting some curiosity, you can initiate some socializing.

CHAPTER 9: Emotional Health

In Chapter 5, we talked about sitting next to your bird's cage for it to become accustomed to your presence. After you've done this, let the bird get used to your hand. Open the cage and simply present your hand. Go slowly because cockatiels are prey animals, so any sudden movement from you may cause them to become fearful. Never grab your bird. That's what a predator would do, and you don't want your cockatiel thinking of your hands as claws or talons.

Now is not the time to try to teach the bird a trick. Keep your voice soft and your demeanor inviting—not demanding. No need to babytalk, though. Merely use your regular speaking voice but in low, gentle tones. Spend time by the open door of the cage. Using that same soft voice, read to the bird. But most of all, be patient and let the bond with your cockatiel develop organically.

HELPFUL TIP
Mirror Mirror

There are some contradictory opinions among cockatiel owners about whether mirrors are beneficial or harmful to birds. Some people believe that lonely cockatiels will become attached to their reflection in the mirror, which can lead to depression. Others consider mirrors enriching toys that can improve the cockatiel's enjoyment of its space. While it's true that solitary cockatiels can become depressed, there is no evidence that mirrors cause cockatiels distress. Since these birds are drawn to shiny surfaces, any number of nonbreakable shiny surfaces can be used as mirror toys, such as tinfoil or a child's plastic mirror toy.

Simple Ways to Encourage Bonding with Your Cockatiel

- Speak in a soft, low voice.
- Be near the cockatiel.
- Offer a favorite food or treat.
- Approach the cage slowly.
- Don't force interactions.
- Don't tower over your cockatiel; stay at eye level.
- Set times for daily interaction.

Cockatiel Behavioral Issues

> "Cockatiels do not bite in nature; their beaks are only used to eat, preen, climb, and build nests. A bird that is biting is either untame, fearful, or has something wrong with it. Do not reward your bird by giving it any attention if it bites—that is what it wants. Ignore the bite and remove the bird for a 'time out.' NEVER scream at the bird, grab its beak, or attempt to punish it for the behavior. Instead, praise the bird for good behavior and give it treats. Be consistent, and the cockatiel will quickly learn that it can't control you and the biting should stop.
>
> BRIDGET MARQUEZ
> *Marquez Tiels*

No two cockatiels are alike. Each will have its own likes and dislikes. To help you better understand some of your bird's behaviors, let's consider body language and what it says about your cockatiel.

Exercise and Affection

Photo Courtesy of Emily Rinearson

It's important to realize cockatiels experience emotions, many of them on par with those of humans. If their mental and emotional state becomes imbalanced, this can lead to physical repercussions. Things like feather picking, screaming, or biting can be signs of boredom. Some cockatiels even climb around their cage in a circle pattern. This is a bird looking for something to do. Give the bird extra attention and as much out-of-cage time as possible. Rotating toys is good for this kind of behavior. It keeps them challenged and entertained. You can also try letting it watch TV or listen to music. They do love to boogie. Exercise and affection play as much of a role in your bird's health as its diet does.

Unfortunately, as with a toddler, birds can't tell us what they're feeling, and these very same behaviors can be the opposite of boredom. Too much stimulation or change in the environment can have the same effect on the cockatiel. Over time, though, you'll learn to recognize your bird's body language and what it's trying to tell you.

Night Frights

> *Cockatiels are more susceptible to suffering from 'night frights' than any other species of bird. They can become easily spooked in darkness and quiet, where any disturbance might send them into a mad frenzy. When your cockatiel has a night fright, calmly turn on the light, uncover the cage, and talk to it soothingly until it visibly calms down. Do not open the cage or attempt to handle your bird in this state. If your bird is still stressed in the morning, keep it quiet and offer it millet, food, and water.*
>
> BRIDGET MARQUEZ
> *Marquez Tiels*

Night frights, or night terrors, are a result of your bird suddenly becoming alarmed or spooked by something in the dark. When the bird reacts to some perceived threat or fear, it will frenetically thrash about the cage and make noise. Night frights are more common in cockatiels than other parrots, and it's not an enjoyable experience for you or your bird. The flight aspect of their "fight or flight" response has taken over.

Unfortunately, there are many things that can trigger a night fright—other animals inside or outside the house, car headlights, shadows, thunderstorms, fireworks, and even new toys placed in the cage right before bedtime. Cockatiels can be spooked by almost anything. But there are some things you can do to help prevent your bird's nocturnal nightmares.

- Furnish the room with blackout curtains or blinds to prevent light and shadow movement in the room.
- Cover half of the cage with a drape (don't hinder ventilation).
- Use a low-level intensity nightlight, so the bird can see.
- From the beginning, help your bird get accustomed to listening to ambient noise nature soundtracks.
- If the bird persists with night frights, examine the room for any new stimulus and remove it if possible.
- You can add a night light and baby monitor (so the bird has a little light to see and a baby monitor so if the cockatiel has become frightened, you will hear and can react).
- Finally, consult your avian vet if you fear something else is going on.

Jealousy

That strong bond you worked so hard to build with your cockatiel can unintentionally cause you a problem. That's because some cockatiels are monogamous and bond with only one person or bird. So, a cockatiel may exhibit unwanted behavior if another person or a new bird is introduced into the home. If you're holding the bird and someone new enters the room, the bird may bite you to try to get you away from that new person. Socializing your bird

CHAPTER 9: Emotional Health

Photo Courtesy of Emily Rinearson

early on can help prevent this. If the bird is used to other people coming and going, it will be less likely to be possessive of you and become more social. You can also have the new person use the same techniques you did to bond with the bird. If the cockatiel is fighting with another bird, house them in separate cages to keep them safe. Then allow them to interact outside the cage, but only at their own pace.

How Your Body Language Can Affect Your Cockatiel

What You Do	Your Cockatiel's Perception
Chasing your cockatiel.	This is predatory behavior and will frighten your bird, which can lead to losing its trust.
Grabbing your cockatiel.	If the situation requires grabbing the bird (vet visit, nail clipping, etc.), wear a glove so the bird won't associate your hand with the action.
Hitting or punishing your bird.	Besides potentially harming the bird, it won't understand the punishment. If discipline is needed, simply walk away from the bird, and it will learn its behavior is associated with your momentarily denying it your attention.
Lying to or teasing your bird with food.	Never cause your bird to lose trust in you by using food to tempt it into good behavior and then not rewarding it with the treat.
Forcing your cockatiel to bathe.	This simply isn't necessary. Cockatiels naturally enjoy bathing and will do so when they're ready.

How to Mentally Stimulate Your Cockatiel

> *It is important to provide your cockatiel with many different toys, as the birds are very smart and love to keep busy. Remember: a bored bird is an unhealthy bird! Having many toys to play with is very stimulating for your little feathery friend, and great for its mental health. Change the toys frequently—you can bring them back again in a week or two so the bird can re-experience them.*
>
> COLLEEN L. RIVAS
> *The Purple Parrot*

CHAPTER 9: Emotional Health

We've touched on toys, but let's break them down some. When you first bring your cockatiel home, and you've gone through the adjustment period and are ready to introduce toys, you'll want to start with something simple. Then, as your bird's curiosity grows, expand into more complicated toys and puzzles. As it learns to play, your cockatiel may pick and choose what it likes. And that's okay. Just have a variety of toys on hand. Here are a few ideas you can use.

Photo Courtesy of Robin Whiteman

- **Chew toys:** Wooden blocks, popsicle sticks on a string, paper shredding toys (may prevent home decor chewing)

- **Preening toys:** Particularly good for single cockatiels, help prevent over-preening of their own feathers

- **Foraging/puzzle toys:** These toys mimic life in the wild and let the bird exercise its ability to look for food.

- **Perch toys:** Swings, ladder & perch combos, playgrounds made of nontoxic materials

- **Edible toys:** Hanging, stacked cuttlebone pieces, edible perches (also made of cuttlebone)

- **Interactive toys:** Plastic ring over a wooden peg, shapes puzzle, food balls

Photo Courtesy of Laura Flanders

There really is no end to what you can use to custom-make your cockatiel's toys. Don't throw away those cardboard egg cartons. Plop some veggies in a few of the compartments and turn it into a toy. Dried orange slices, dried pasta, and wooden spools are simple toys that require no added expense. Wads of paper with bits of food hidden inside. Make it more complicated and put a piece of food inside a small wad of paper and then place that inside a larger piece of wadded paper. You've just made your own puzzle toy. As you design and create your bird's toys, be sure to avoid toxic materials. No lead, plastic that could be ingested, or anything they could chew the paint off. Safety, safety, safety.

Traveling

It's not advised that you travel with your new cockatiel. As you've read so far, there are a lot of things to consider when helping a cockatiel adjust to its new environment. Traveling could break any routines you are working to establish. If you need to travel and simply can't leave the bird at home, talk with your vet and get any advice they have to offer. Just remember, you've taken a lot of time and care to make your home a safe environment for your bird. A hotel or Airbnb most likely will not have done the same.

If you do need to travel with your cockatiel, there is training called crate training that can be done. This training can assist with traveling to the vet or to new locations. You can reach out to a professional certified parrot behavior consultant/trainer to assist with crate training.

How to Show Your Affection

> *Cockatiels tend to love riding around on our shoulders and hanging out with us. They also like sitting on our fingers and 'talking' to us. Most of all, they love being active parts of our lives and NOT just sitting in their cages all day. In fact, I've known many people who leave the cage door open throughout the day so the bird can come and go as it wishes!*
>
> **DANA GRIMM**
> *Beaks and Tweets Aviary*

Photo Courtesy of Kim O'Toole

By taking the steps to bond with your bird that we've covered in this book, you'll be letting the bird make the first move. This will build its confidence and courage. And over time, you will learn what your bird likes and doesn't like from you in the form of attention and affection, especially as you learn to interpret its body language.

When your bird has learned to trust you and step up when commanded, you can start to try petting it. Cockatiels love being rubbed behind the crest. It will even beg for a little nuzzle at times. But, again, take your cues from the bird, and you'll find what works best for you both.

How a Cockatiel Shows Its Affection

A cockatiel's body language will give you an indication of how it is feeling.

- Chirps at your approach
- Has warm feet
- Body is relaxed
- Crest feathers are curved slightly upward
- Smooths feathers
- Tail wags and eyes blink incessantly
- Trots toward you with head held high

CHAPTER 9: Emotional Health

Interpreting Sounds

The sounds your cockatiel makes can also help you understand what it is experiencing. They use a variety of sounds to communicate their intentions. Here's how to recognize what these different sounds can mean.

- Contact call or flock call: This is just your bird keeping track of you as part of its flock. You can answer back with a simple, "I'm here."
- Screams: These sounds are used to get attention. It could mean the bird is lonely, sad, scared, or upset.
- Chirping: Cockatiels chirp when they are content and want to let you know you're a part of the flock. They will also chirp when curious and inquisitive.
- Hissing: If your cockatiel is angry or feels threatened, it will hiss, even at you. These are short bursts that are really kind of cute.
- Beak grinding: This is similar to a cat purring in that it's a sign of contentment. A bird will sometimes do it when being petted.
- Whistling: Males tend to whistle more than females, and they can be incessant at times. It's still cute, though!
- Mimicking: As with whistling, males mimic more often than females do. And though it sounds like your bird is talking to you, it's merely mimicking the sounds you make.

CHAPTER 10

Training Essentials

Why Is Training Important?

When your cockatiel comes home, it can be extremely exciting having all these expectations for your new pet. As this wonderful cockatiel is getting adjusted to the unfamiliar environment, we need to remember this cockatiel is not a cat or a dog. The cockatiel may not be ready to be touched or to immediately interact with you. The cockatiel could appear scared (backs away) when you approach the cage or when you attempt to take it out of the cage. Do not take it personally. Your cockatiel needs time to adjust and build trust with you.

Photo Courtesy of Kim O'Toole

Through training, you will develop a mutually trusting partnership. Training is not all about teaching your cockatiel tricks. Training is about building trust. Training is very important for the cockatiel's quality of life by encouraging choice, problem-solving, and positive interaction with humans. By taking the time to understand your cockatiel's body language, you will avoid forcing or pushing the bird into an uncomfortable situation.

Once your cockatiel has settled into the cage, this is when

training begins. Remember: the cockatiel is in a new environment and does not understand everything going on.

- During the first couple of days, give your cockatiel space. Do not hover over the cockatiel (do not be a hawk).
- Do not feel obligated to let the cockatiel out of the cage. Letting a cockatiel out of the cage too soon could lead to the cockatiel getting injured or to you having to chase and capture the bird to place back in the cage, which can cause stress.
- You can sit in the room, but not right next to the cage. Enjoy just sitting in the room, watching how your cockatiel interacts with the items in the cage.

Understanding the Training Methodology

Training presented in this chapter will be broken up into step-by-step segments to assist with success stages to get to the end training goal. The chapter training will follow the science studies from B. F. Skinner's book *Science and Human Behavior* and Paul Chance's *Learning and Behavior*. The references build the practices of force-free and less intrusive, minimally aversive (LIMA) process methodology. This methodology avoids using force and fear in trying to teach a behavior.

You may have heard the term "positive reinforcement" on social media or in a training article. Maybe you have heard other phrases that are associated with positive reinforcement, terms such as reward-based training and choice training. When people hear these terms, there is a misconception that the training is just giving the animal treats all the time. "Reward-based learning offers the most advantages and is least harmful to the learner's welfare." This is why it is important to understand what positive reinforcement is and how it can work.

Positive reinforcement means that **adding** (+ *positive*) a high-value reinforcer (food, scratches, toy, attention, etc.) immediately after a desired behavior may **increase or maintain** the likelihood of that **behavior** occurring (*reinforcement*).

This training methodology creates a learning consequence loop for the cockatiel and you.

For example,

Setting up the environment: The cockatiel is in the cage.

Antecedent (the action before the behavior): You slowly approach the cage.

Behavior (the behavior): The cockatiel moves toward the food bowl.

Consequence (the action after the behavior): You place a small amount of millet in the food bowl.

Prediction: The cockatiel will continue to go to the food bowl when you approach the cage. The behavior of the cockatiel going to the food bowl is **reinforced** by **adding** the millet to the food bowl.

As long as this predictable event continues every time (history of events), the cockatiel will continue to approach the food bowl (or may approach the food bowl before you get there), thus creating a learning consequence loop. By incorporating this approach, your cockatiel will be more interested in working with you and reduce the chances of your cockatiel learning to nip or bite.

There are two takeaways from this training example:

- It encourages new trainable behavior and gives the cockatiel the opportunity to choose to engage.
- It builds trust with small incremental steps (not force or expectations).

With any training, you want to ensure the following:

- You are not taking too big of a step at once.
- Your cockatiel picks the reinforcer (not you).
- You do not make the training sessions too long.
- Watch the cockatiel's behavior so as to not push the bird into a fear response.
- You are not accidentally reinforcing the incorrect behavior.
  - For Example:

CHAPTER 10: Training Essentials

- Antecedent (the action before the behavior): You are talking in another room.
- Behavior (the behavior): The cockatiel starts making noise.
- Consequence (the action after the behavior): You come into the room to check on the cockatiel.
- Prediction: The cockatiel will continue to make noise when you are talking in another room. The behavior of the cockatiel making noise is **reinforced** by **adding** your appearance in the room.

The Basics

Before starting any training, it is important to find out your cockatiel's favorite motivation (reinforcer). When your cockatiel is in the cage, you should observe the bird's activities—seeking out specific food items in the food bowl, singing/whistling/talking for attention, destroying specific toys, and/or lowering the head for scratches.

If you are not sure of your cockatiel's favorite motivation, start by observing the food bowl; what does your cockatiel eat first and second? When you can identify those favorite food items, remove them from the daily food bowl and use them for training. That is your first step toward training.

Introduction Training

The basic introduction training starts after you have set up the cage, have placed the cockatiel in the cage, and are checking on the bird in the cage.

1. Put a small amount of the cockatiel's favorite food item (a small amount of millet or crumbled pieces of avicake or nutraberry) in your hand before you approach the cage.
2. Walk slowly toward the cage. As you approach, start to observe the cockatiel's body language:

- If the cockatiel starts to move toward the back of the cage or is pacing on and off the cage bars or perch, stop moving and wait. Once the cockatiel stops moving, move slowly toward the front of the cage.
- If the cockatiel continues to move or pace, turn around and leave. Try again later (and slow your pace more).
3. When the cockatiel has settled in a location in the cage, continue to slowly approach, and as you get to the front of the cage, drop/place the favorite food item into the food bowl and then walk away.

When doing these steps slowly over time, continue to watch the cockatiel's body behavior (moving away or toward you). Over time, the cockatiel may start approaching the food bowl to greet you to receive the favorite items.

Have patience, remember to do the training slowly (try not to rush the cage), and save those favorite items for training. (Don't feed them daily to the cockatiel in the cage.) Practice when you can, provide the bird with space, and the desired behavior will occur.

The keys to training:

- Before starting any training, discover what your cockatiel likes to eat.
- You should be in the mood to train, and your cockatiel must be interested in interacting.
- Remember how to set up training expectations through patience, planning, and practice.
- Training reduces boredom and undesired behavior.
- Training encourages choice, problem-solving, and positive consequences with the bird's humans.

The next sections will cover specific topics on Target Training, Station Training, and Stepping Up Training. These introduction trainings will build confidence and human/avian bonding as well as assist in vet care. In the next sections, you can use a clicker when you say the word "Good." The sound of a clicker or the word "Good" are markers to tell the cockatiel this is the trained behavior. If you have a soft clicker, then use just one click. During some training sessions, you may not have the clicker on you, or you may not own a clicker. Then just use the verbal marker "good" when you see the achieved behavior.

Target Training

Target training is an important skill for a cockatiel to learn. This teaches the cockatiel to target the tip of a target stick with its beak. This training has the following benefits:

- It assists with a cockatiel that is nervous about hands or has a history of biting. Target training is hands-off training (you are not touching the cockatiel).
- It increases the cockatiel's confidence by teaching the bird what it can do to earn attention and positive feedback.
- It helps the bird move toward veterinary care training, such as going into the crate and taking medication.

The small incremental steps below build to the final goal of target training. The objective of each step is to only move forward when the cockatiel appears comfortable and accepts the food item (or attention/scratches).

The incremental steps give your cockatiel the ability to choose to engage in the training session (empowerment). Usually, after the sessions, the cockatiel may appear tired (which is normal). Training can be very enriching for companion cockatiels.

Setting up the Environment

Supplies needed:
- Target stick – chopstick, empty plastic pen, small branch 6- to 8-inches long, professional target stick (not too big)
- Bird's favorite food

Before you start training

1. The human needs to be in the mood to train. If you are not in a happy-go-lucky mood, do not train. Cockatiels can read our body language better than we can. If your cockatiel observes sluggish or "whatever" human body language, the bird may not train.
2. Make sure that the cockatiel has had several hours of not eating its favorite food item.
3. Have a couple of the bird's favorite food items in your back pocket or in the palm of your hand so the cockatiel is focused on you and not the yummy item. We do not want to cue the cockatiel that you have the yummy items. (I would recommend four to six broken pieces of the yummy items so you can do several repetitions of the steps.)
4. Ensure the cockatiel is in the cage (and not all worked up) to start.

NOTE:

Each step should take no more than a minute. Do not rush it. Track/observe the cockatiel's body language, and only move to the next step when the body language appears calm and the bird is interested in eating.

CHAPTER 10: Training Essentials

Shaping Training toward Target Training

Shaping Flowing toward Target Training

Incremental Step 1 ▸ Desensitization of Target Stick

This is the beginner step to start to teach the cockatiel that when the target stick appears, food will be delivered.

1. The cockatiel should be in the cage.
2. You should stand about three feet away from the front of the cage.
   - Hold the target stick behind your back in one hand. The yummy item will be in your other hand (not visible to the cockatiel). Yes, there is some coordination needed.
3. As you are standing three feet away from the cage, slowly move the target stick from behind you to directly in front of you. (And I mean *slowly,* almost creepily, move your hand with the target stick. Count one–one thousand, etc., as you move it. Slow is key.)
   - You do not have to say anything.
   - Do not wiggle the stick. You really want it not to be a big deal for the bird.
4. Observe the cockatiel's body language before proceeding.

If the cockatiel is not screaming, squawking, pacing, flying, flopping to the bottom of the cage, or freaking out, all other behavior will be considered calm behavior.

 **PROCEED:**

   i. Say "Good," and remember to PRAISE, PRAISE. This is the cue that this is the behavior you want to see, and you are ending the session. Anything that happens after this point does not matter.
   ii. Move the target stick behind you (or place it on the floor).
   iii. While the target stick is behind you or on the floor, walk slowly up to the cockatiel's cage and drop a piece of yummy food into the bowl. Or, if you can (carefully) hand-feed the cockatiel, do so with your hand directly in front of the bird.

If the cockatiel is screaming, squawking, pacing, or has feathers all fluffed, this means the cockatiel is not comfortable with your movement and is having a fear response:

 DO NOT PROCEED:

   i. Wait until the cockatiel's behavior settles down.
      - If the cockatiel's behavior settles down quickly, take a step back and go back to step 3. Try another attempt at training.
      - If the cockatiel's behavior does not settle down quickly, end the session (no treat is given).
   ii. During the next repetition, back up another foot or make the target stick shorter, and that will be your new starting point. (Mark how far away you are from the cockatiel).

5. Go back to Step 3 and do one repetition, then take a break.

You can do this step several times a day. As long as the cockatiel shows calm behavior through several training repetitions, then you can move to the next incremental step.

Don't rush it; every cockatiel learns differently. Go at your cockatiel's pace.

CHAPTER 10: Training Essentials

Incremental Step 2 ▶ Desensitization of a Target Stick (Closer)

This next step continues to teach the cockatiel that when the target stick appears, food will be delivered.

1. The cockatiel should be in the cage.
2. You should stand about two feet away from the front of the cage.
   - The target stick should be behind you, held behind your back in one hand. The yummy item should be in the other hand.
3. As you are standing two feet away from the cage, slowly move the target stick (*slowly*) from behind you to directly in front of you.
   - You do not have to say anything.
   - Do not wiggle the stick. You really want it to not be a big deal to the bird.
4. Observe the cockatiel's body language before proceeding.

If the cockatiel is not screaming, squawking, pacing, flying, flopping to the bottom of the cage, or freaking out:

 PROCEED:

   i. Say "Good," and remember to PRAISE, PRAISE. (This is the cue that this is the behavior you want to see, and you are ending the session. Anything that happens after this point does not matter.)
   ii. Move the target stick behind you (or place it on the floor).
   iii. While the target stick is behind you or on the floor, walk slowly up to the cockatiel's cage and drop a piece of yummy food into the bowl. Or, if you can (carefully) hand-feed the cockatiel, do so with your hand directly in front of the bird.

If the cockatiel is screaming, squawking, pacing, or the feathers are all fluffed up:

 DO NOT PROCEED:

   i. Wait until the cockatiel's behavior settles down.
       - If the cockatiel's behavior settles down quickly, take a step back, go back to Step 3, and try another attempt at the training.
       - If the cockatiel's behavior does not settle down quickly, end the session (no treat is given).
   ii. During the next repetition, go back to **Incremental Step 1**. Do a few more repetitions at **Incremental Step 1**.

5. Go back to Step 2 and do one repetition, and then take a break.

You can do this step several times a day. As long as the cockatiel shows calm behavior throughout several training repetitions, you can move to the next incremental step.

Don't rush it; every cockatiel learns differently. Go at your cockatiel's pace.

Incremental Step 3 ▶ Desensitization of a Target Stick (Near the Cage)

Each of these steps guides the cockatiel toward feeling comfortable touching the target stick.

1. The cockatiel should be in the cage.
2. You should be standing about one foot away from the front of the cage.
   - The target stick will be behind you, held behind your back in one hand. The yummy item should be in the other hand.
3. As you are standing one foot away from the cage, slowly move the target stick from behind you to directly in front of you.

4. This is the tricky part. Move the stick so the tip of the target stick points in high. Point and angle up slowly as you move the target stick toward the cage (but not into the cage barring and about several inches from the cage).
5. Observe the cockatiel's body language before proceeding.

If the cockatiel is not screaming, squawking, pacing, flying, flopping to the bottom of the cage, or freaking out:

 PROCEED:

   i. Say "Good," and remember to PRAISE, PRAISE. This is the cue that this is the behavior you want to see, and you are ending the session. Anything that happens after this point does not matter.
   ii. Move the target stick behind you (or place it on the floor).
   iii. While the target stick is behind you or on the floor, walk slowly up to the cockatiel's cage and drop a piece of yummy food into the food bowl. Or, if you can (carefully) hand-feed the cockatiel, do so with your hand directly in front of the bird.

If the cockatiel is screaming, squawking, pacing, or the feathers are all fluffed up:

 DO NOT PROCEED:

   i. Wait until the cockatiel's behavior settles down.
      - If the cockatiel's behavior settles down quickly, take a step back, go back to Step 3, and try another attempt at the training.
   ii. If the cockatiel's behavior does not settle down quickly, end the session (no treat is given).

During the next repetition, go back to **Incremental Step 2**. Do a few more repetitions of **Incremental Step 2**.

6. Go back to Step 2 and do one repetition, then take a break.

You can do this step several times a day. As long as the cockatiel shows calm behavior throughout several training repetitions, move to the next incremental step.

Don't rush it; every cockatiel learns differently. Go at your cockatiel's pace.

Incremental Step 04 ▶ Touch the Target Stick

Each of these steps guides the cockatiel toward touching the target stick.

1. The cockatiel should be in the cage.
2. You should stand about one foot or a tad closer to the front of the cage.
   - The target stick should be behind you, held behind your back in one hand. The yummy item should be in the other hand.
3. As you are standing one foot away from the cage, slowly move the target stick from behind you to directly in front of you.
4. This is the tricky part. As you move the target stick closer to the bird, instead of the target stick be held straight in front of you, try to angle the target stick tip at an angle toward the cage near the bird (but not into the cage barring and about several inches from the cage).

CHAPTER 10: Training Essentials

Try to move the target stick tip close to the cage bars, but don't slide the stick in. Move it just far enough that the cockatiel can reach the target stick with the beak.

If the cockatiel is not screaming, squawking, pacing, flying, flopping to the bottom of the cage, or freaking out,

- Wait about one to two seconds to see if one of these behaviors occurs:
    - The cockatiel moves toward the tip of the target stick (but may not be trying to touch it).
    - The cockatiel attempts to move its beak between the bars to touch the target stick.
    - The cockatiel slowly taps the top of the target stick with the beak. (Try to avoid the cockatiel attempting to bite the target stick; the goal is just to have the cockatiel tap the target with its beak.)
- If the cockatiel **does exhibit any** of the above behaviors:

 PROCEED:
    i. Say "Good," and remember to PRAISE, PRAISE. This is the cue that this is the behavior you want to see, and you are ending the session. Anything that happens after this point does not matter.
    ii. Move the target stick behind you (or place it on the floor).
    iii. While the target stick is behind you or on the floor, walk slowly up to the cockatiel's cage and drop a piece of yummy food into the food bowl. Or, if you can (carefully) hand-feed the cockatiel, do so with your hand directly in front of the bird.

If the cockatiel is screaming, squawking, pacing, or the feathers are all fluffed up:

 DO NOT PROCEED:
    i. Wait until the cockatiel's behavior settles down.
        - If the cockatiel's behavior settles down quickly,

take a step back, go back to Step 3, and try another attempt at the training.
- If the cockatiel's behavior does not settle down quickly, end the session (no treat is given).

ii. During the next repetition, go back to **Incremental Step 3**. Do a few more repetitions of **Incremental Step 3**.

ADDITIONAL STEP

If the cockatiel bites the target stick or takes the target stick,

i. Let the target stick go. The cockatiel will drop the stick to the bottom of the cage.
ii. Go back to **Incremental Step 3** for a couple more days and then move to **Incremental Step 4**.

You can do this step several times a day. As long as the cockatiel shows calm behavior throughout several training repetitions, you can move to the next step.

Don't rush it; every cockatiel learns differently. Go at your cockatiel's pace. All of this training creates fluency and successful learning.

 ## Putting It All Together: Goal Target Training

Before you start training

1. The human needs to be in the mood to train. If you are not in a happy-go-lucky mood, do not train. Cockatiels can read our body language better than we can. If your cockatiel observes sluggish or "whatever" human body language, the bird may not train.
2. Make sure that the cockatiel has had several hours of not eating its favorite food item.
3. Have a couple of the bird's favorite food items in your back pocket or in the palm of your hand so the cockatiel is focused on you and not the yummy item. We do not want to cue the cockatiel that you have the yummy items. (I would recommend four to six broken

CHAPTER 10: Training Essentials

pieces of the yummy items so you can do several repetitions of the steps.)
4. Ensure the cockatiel is in the cage (and not all worked up) to start.

NOTE:

Each step should take no more than a minute. Do not rush it. Track/observe the cockatiel's body language, and only move to the next step when the body language appears calm and the bird is interested in eating.

Putting it all together session:

1. The cockatiel should be in the cage.
2. You should be standing about one foot or a tad closer to the front of the cage.
   - The target stick should be behind you, held behind your back in one hand. The yummy item should be in the other hand.

3. As you are standing one foot away from the cage, slowly move the target stick from behind you to directly in front of you, and slowly move the target stick to within half an inch of the outside of the cage.
    - Try to move the stick close to the cage bars, just far enough so the cockatiel can reach the stick with its beak.

If the cockatiel is not screaming, squawking, pacing, flying, flopping to the bottom of the cage, or freaking out:

- Say "Touch" to now train the cockatiel with a cue word for this newly learned behavior.
- Now wait about one to two seconds to see if one of these behaviors occurs:
    - The cockatiel moves toward the tip of the target stick (but may not be trying to touch it).
    - The cockatiel attempts to move its beak between the bars to touch the target stick.

    - The cockatiel slowly taps the top of its beak to the stick. (Try to avoid the cockatiel attempting to bite the target stick; the goal is just to have the cockatiel tap the target with its beak.)
- If the cockatiel does exhibit **any** of the above behaviors:

CHAPTER 10: Training Essentials

 **PROCEED:**

i. Say "Good," and remember to PRAISE, PRAISE. This is the cue that this is the behavior you want to see, and you are ending the session. Anything that happens after this point does not matter.
ii. Move the target stick behind you (or place it on the floor).
iii. While the target stick is behind you or on the floor, walk slowly up to the cockatiel's cage and drop a piece of yummy food into the food bowl. Or, if you can (carefully) hand-feed the cockatiel, do so with your hand directly in front of the bird.

If the cockatiel is screaming, squawking, pacing, or the feathers are all fluffed up:

 DO NOT PROCEED:

i. Wait until the cockatiel's behavior settles down.
   - If the cockatiel's behavior settles down quickly, take a step back, go back to Step 3, and try another attempt at the training.
   - If the cockatiel's behavior does not settle down quickly, end the session (no treat is given).
ii. During the next repetition, go back to **Incremental Step 3**. Do a few more repetitions of **Incremental Step 3**.

Once the cockatiel has completed one repetition, try to do one more session and then end the training.

Practice these incremental steps for the cockatiel to become fluent and confident in the newly learned behavior. If the cockatiel seems to have forgotten a step, go back a few steps to build confidence.

Don't rush it; every cockatiel learns differently. Go at your cockatiel's pace.

Once the cockatiel is an expert at touching the target, you can try to move the target stick to another location about six inches away from your original location. Again, if the cockatiel is having trouble understanding the request, use all the incremental steps to reteach the bird to target the stick in a new location. Every new location is a new training situation for the cockatiel to relearn the new behavior. Over time, the cockatiel will learn that target training can happen anywhere.

Station Training

Station training is an important skill to teach the cockatiel to learn to stay at a location for a short duration.

- If you open the cage door, you do not want the cockatiel to fly out. Instead, you want the cockatiel to stay in a specific location (like a perch in the cage).
- When the cockatiel is out of the cage, this can be associated with target training to move the cockatiel back into the cage.
- Station training can lead to training the bird to step up on a hand, perch, cockatiel ladder, or a perch on a scale at the veterinarian's office.

Setting up the Environment

Supplies needed

- Identified favorite food items
- A perch placed on the inside of the cage door or in close proximity to the cage door
- A small dish to be placed next to the perch

Before you start the training

1. The human needs to be in the mood to train. If you are not in a happy-go-lucky mood, do not train. Cockatiels can read our body language better than we can. If your cockatiel observes sluggish or "whatever" human body language, the bird may not train.

CHAPTER 10: Training Essentials

2. Make sure that the cockatiel has had several hours of not eating the favorite food item.
3. Have a couple of the bird's favorite food items in your back pocket or in the palm of your hand so the cockatiel is focused on you and not the yummy item. We do not want to cue the cockatiel that you have the yummy items. (I would recommend four to six broken pieces of the yummy items so you can do several repetitions of the steps.)
4. Ensure the cockatiel is in the cage (and not all worked up) to start.

NOTE:

Each step should take no more than a minute. Do not rush it. Track/observe the cockatiel's body language, and only move to the next step when the body language appears calm and the bird is interested in eating.

Shaping toward Stationing Behavior

Incremental Step 01 Identifying a Perch

This is the beginner step to teach the cockatiel to go to a specific perch inside of the cage door or a perch near the cage door so a yummy treat will be delivered.

1. The cockatiel should be in the cage.
2. You should be standing about one foot away from the cage.
    i. Make sure the yummy item is hidden in your hand.
3. Slowly approach the cage.

If the cockatiel is not screaming, squawking, pacing, flying, flopping to the bottom of the cage, or freaking out:

 PROCEED: Go to Step 4.

If the cockatiel is screaming, squawking, pacing, or its feathers are all fluffed up:

 DO NOT PROCEED:

  i. Wait until the cockatiel's behavior settles down.
     - If the cockatiel's behavior settles down quickly, take a step back, and try another attempt at the training (slow down your pace).
     - If the cockatiel's behavior does not settle down quickly, end the session (no treat is given).

4. Once you are in front of the cage,
    i. Show the yummy food item near the perch inside the cage for about one to two seconds to lure the cockatiel toward the perch.

If the cockatiel is not screaming, squawking, pacing, flying, flopping to the bottom of the cage, or freaking out:

 PROCEED: Go to Step 5.

CHAPTER 10: Training Essentials

If the cockatiel is screaming, squawking, pacing, or its feathers are all fluffed up:

 DO NOT PROCEED:

    i. Wait until the cockatiel's behavior settles down.
- If the cockatiel's behavior settles down quickly, take a step back, and try another attempt at the training (slow down your pace).
- If the cockatiel's behavior does not settle down quickly, end the session (no treat is given).

5. Place the yummy item in the bowl by the perch and back up.
6. Watch to see when the cockatiel touches the perch with one foot (usually when the cockatiel goes to get the yummy item).

    i. Say "Good," or PRAISE, PRAISE. (Yes, this seems backward, but we are capturing the behavior when the cockatiel touches the perch.)
    ii. If the cockatiel does not go to the dish within 30 seconds, make sure you have identified this as a favorite item, and the cockatiel has not had this food for several hours. Try again later in the day or the next day.

7. When the cockatiel is done eating the food, see if the bird leaves the perch.
- When the cockatiel leaves the perch, try to do one more repetition (go back to step 2) and then end the session.

NOTE:

Try to do this session once or twice a day, if possible. If you can do this session several times a day, and you see the cockatiel is showing calm behavior throughout the session and is moving to the perch faster, you can move to the next incremental step.

Incremental Step 2 ▷ Reinforcing Going to the Perch

This is the next step to teach the cockatiel to go to a specific perch so a yummy treat will be delivered.

1. The cockatiel should be in the cage.
2. You should be standing about one foot away from the cage.
    i. Make sure the yummy item is hidden in your hand.
3. Slowly approach the cage.

If the cockatiel is not screaming, squawking, pacing, flying, flopping to the bottom of the cage, or freaking out,

 PROCEED: Go to Step 4.

If the cockatiel is screaming, squawking, pacing, or the feathers are all fluffed up,

 DO NOT PROCEED:

   i. Wait until the cockatiel's behavior settles down.
      - If the cockatiel's behavior settles down quickly, take a step back, and try another attempt at the training (slow down your pace).
      - If the cockatiel's behavior does not settle down quickly, end the session (no treat is given).
4. Once you are in front of the cage, tap your finger once by the designated perch from outside the cage, cueing the stationing behavior.

CHAPTER 10: Training Essentials

    i. Do not show the yummy item (we want to fade out the lure).
    ii. If the cockatiel does not come over, then show the yummy food item by the perch for about one to two seconds to lure the cockatiel toward the perch. For each repetition, try not to show the food item; only lure if the cockatiel needs a little assistance to remember the training.

If the cockatiel is not screaming, squawking, pacing, flying, flopping to the bottom of the cage, or freaking out:

 PROCEED: Go to Step 5.

If the cockatiel is screaming, squawking, pacing, or its feathers are all fluffed up:

 DO NOT PROCEED:

    i. Wait until the cockatiel's behavior settles down.
        • If the cockatiel's behavior settles down quickly, take a step back, and try another attempt at the training (slow down your pace).

        • If the cockatiel's behavior does not settle down quickly, end the session (no treat is given).

5. When the cockatiel comes to the perch, wait until you see two feet are on the perch (even for a second).
    i. Say "Good," or PRAISE, PRAISE.
    ii. Either directly give the yummy item to the cockatiel or place the yummy item in the bowl by the perch.
    iii. If the cockatiel does not go to the dish within 30 seconds, make sure this is a favorite item and the cockatiel has not had this food for several hours. Try again later in the day or the next day, or go back to **Incremental Step 1** (for Stationing).
6. When the cockatiel is done eating, see if the bird leaves the perch.
    - When the cockatiel leaves the perch, try to do one more repetition (go back to step 2), and then end the session.

Incremental Step 3 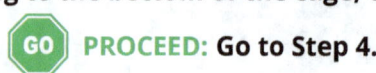 Stationing to the Perch (duration)

The next step is to teach the cockatiel to go to a specific perch on the inside of the cage door or a perch near the cage door and stay for a second so a yummy treat will be delivered. The objective of this step is to teach the cockatiel to stay in a location.

1. The cockatiel should be in the cage.
2. You should be standing about one foot away from the cage.
    - Make sure the yummy item is hidden in your hand.
3. Slowly approach the cage.

If the cockatiel is not screaming, squawking, pacing, flying, flopping to the bottom of the cage, or freaking out:

GO **PROCEED: Go to Step 4.**

CHAPTER 10: Training Essentials

If the cockatiel is screaming, squawking, pacing, or the feathers are all fluffed up:

 DO NOT PROCEED:

    i. Wait until the cockatiel's behavior settles down.
- If the cockatiel's behavior settles down quickly, take a step back, and try another attempt at the training (slow down your pace).
- If the cockatiel's behavior does not settle down quickly, end the session (no treat is given).

4. Once you are in front of the cage, tap your finger once by the designated perch, cueing the stationing behavior.
   i. Do not show the yummy item (we want to fade out the lure).
   ii. If the cockatiel does not come over, go back to **Incremental Step 1** or **Incremental Step 2**.

If the cockatiel is not screaming, squawking, pacing, flying, flopping to the bottom of the cage, or freaking out:

 PROCEED: Go to Step 5.

If the cockatiel is screaming, squawking, pacing, or the feathers are all fluffed up:

 DO NOT PROCEED:

    i. Wait until the cockatiel's behavior settles down.
- If the cockatiel's behavior settles down quickly, take

NOTE:

Try to do this session once or twice a day, if possible. If you can do this session several times a day, and you see the cockatiel is showing calm behavior throughout the session and is moving to the perch faster, you can move to the next step.

a step back, and try another attempt at the training (slow down your pace).
  - If the cockatiel's behavior does not settle down quickly, end the session (no treat is given).
5. When the cockatiel comes to the perch, wait until two feet are on the perch and count one–one thousand.
    i. Say "Good," or PRAISE, PRAISE.
    ii. Either directly give the yummy item to the cockatiel or place the yummy item in the bowl by the perch.
    iii. If the cockatiel does not go to the dish within 30 seconds, make sure you have identified this is a favorite item and the cockatiel has not had this food for several hours. Try again later in the day or the next day, or go back to **Incremental Step 1 (for Stationing)**.
6. When the cockatiel is done eating the food, see if the bird leaves the perch.
    - When the cockatiel leaves the perch, try to do one more repetition (go back to step 2), and then end the session.

NOTE:

Try to do this session once or twice a day, if possible. If you can do this session several times a day, and you see the cockatiel is showing calm behavior throughout the session and is moving to the perch faster, you can move to the next incremental step.

After several successful repetitions, add an additional second to this training session. Practice getting the cockatiel to station on the perch for 10 seconds.

CHAPTER 10: Training Essentials

Incremental Step 04 ▶ Stationing to the Perch (duration/and working toward opening the cage door)

1. The cockatiel should be in the cage.
2. You should be standing about one foot away from the cage.
   - Make sure the yummy item is hidden in your hand.
3. Slowly approach the cage.

If the cockatiel **is not** screaming, squawking, pacing, flying, flopping to the bottom of the cage, or freaking out:

 PROCEED: Go to Step 4.

If the cockatiel **is** screaming, squawking, pacing, or the feathers are all fluffed up:

 DO NOT PROCEED:

   i. Wait until the cockatiel's behavior settles down.
      - If the cockatiel's behavior settles down quickly, take a step back, and try another attempt at the training (slow down your pace).
      - If the cockatiel's behavior does not settle down quickly, end the session (no treat is given).

4. Once you are in front of the cage, tap your finger once by the designated perch, cueing the stationing behavior.
   i. Do not show the yummy item (we want to fade out the lure).
   ii. If the cockatiel does not come over, go back to **Incremental Step 1** or **Incremental Step 2**.

If the cockatiel **is not** screaming, squawking, pacing, flying, flopping to the bottom of the cage, or freaking out:

 PROCEED: Go to Step 5.

If the cockatiel is screaming, squawking, pacing, or the feathers are all fluffed up:

 DO NOT PROCEED:

    i. Wait until the cockatiel's behavior settles down.
- If the cockatiel's behavior settles down quickly, take a step back, and try another attempt at the training (slow down your pace).
- If the cockatiel's behavior does not settle down quickly, end the session (no treat is given).

5. When the cockatiel comes to the perch, wait until two feet are on the perch and just touch the cage door lock.
    i. If the cockatiel stays on the perch
    - Say "Good," or PRAISE, PRAISE.
    - Either directly give the yummy item to the cockatiel or place the yummy item in the bowl by the perch.
    - Go to step 6.
    ii. If the cockatiel does not stay on the perch
    - Go back to **Incremental Step 3: Stationing to the perch (duration)** and work on more repetitions.

6. When the cockatiel is done eating, see if it leaves the perch.
    - When the cockatiel leaves the perch, try to do one more repetition (go back to step 2), and then end the session.

 **NOTE:**

Try to do this session once or twice a day, if possible. If you can do this session several times a day, and you see the cockatiel is showing calm behavior throughout the session and is moving to the perch faster, you can move to the next incremental step.

CHAPTER 10: Training Essentials

Incremental Step 5 ▶ **Stationing to the Perch (duration/ and working toward opening the cage door)**

1. The cockatiel should be in the cage.
2. You should be standing about one foot away from the cage.
    i. Make sure the yummy item is hidden in your hand.
3. Slowly approach the front of the cage and tap your finger once by the designated perch, cueing the stationing behavior.
    i. Do not show the yummy item (we want to fade out the lure).

If the cockatiel is not screaming, squawking, pacing, flying, flopping to the bottom of the cage, or freaking out:

 PROCEED: Go to Step 4.

If the cockatiel is screaming, squawking, pacing, or the feathers are all fluffed up:

 DO NOT PROCEED:

   i. Wait until the cockatiel's behavior settles down.
      - If the cockatiel's behavior settles down quickly, take a step back, and try another attempt at the training (slow down your pace).

- If the cockatiel's behavior does not settle down quickly, end the session (no treat is given).

4. When the cockatiel comes to the perch, wait until two feet are on the perch, touch the lock, and slowly unlock and relock the door.

   i. If the cockatiel stays on the perch
      - Say "Good," or PRAISE, PRAISE.
      - Either directly give the yummy item to the cockatiel or place the yummy item in the bowl by the perch.
      - Go to step 5.
   ii. If the cockatiel does not stay on the perch
      - Go back to **Incremental Step 3: Stationing to the Perch**, and work on more repetitions.

5. When the cockatiel is done eating, see if the bird leaves the perch.
   - When the cockatiel leaves the perch, try to do one more repetition (go back to step 2) and then end the session.

NOTE:

Try to do this session once or twice a day, if possible. If you can do this session several times a day, and you see the cockatiel is showing calm behavior throughout the session and is moving to the perch faster, you can move to the next incremental step.

CHAPTER 10: Training Essentials

Incremental Step 6 ▶ Stationing to the Perch (working toward opening the cage door)

1. The cockatiel should be in the cage.
2. You should be standing about one foot away from the cage.
    i. Make sure the yummy item is hidden in your hand.

3. Slowly approach the front of the cage and tap your finger once by the designated perch, cueing the stationing behavior.
    i. Do not show the yummy item (we want to fade out the lure).

If the cockatiel is not screaming, squawking, pacing, flying, flopping to the bottom of the cage, or freaking out:

 PROCEED: Go to Step 5.

If the cockatiel is screaming, squawking, pacing, or the feathers are all fluffed up:

 DO NOT PROCEED:

  i. Wait until the cockatiel's behavior settles down.
   - If the cockatiel's behavior settles down quickly, take a step back, and try another attempt at the training (slow down your pace).
   - If the cockatiel's behavior does not settle down quickly, end the session (no treat is given).

4. When the cockatiel comes to the perch, wait until two feet are on the perch, then touch the lock. Slowly unlock the door, and open the cage door only an inch (so the cockatiel cannot escape). Wait for one second and relock the door.
    i. If the cockatiel stays on the perch
      - Say "Good," or PRAISE, PRAISE.
      - Either directly give the yummy item to the cockatiel or place the yummy item in the bowl by the perch.
      - Go to step 6.
    ii. If the cockatiel does not stay on the perch

- Go back to **Incremental Step 5: Stationing to the Perch (duration)** and work on more repetitions.
5. When the cockatiel is done eating, see if the bird leaves the perch.
   - When the cockatiel leaves the perch, try to do one more repetition (go back to step 2), and then end the session.

NOTE:

Try to do this session once or twice a day, if possible. If you can do this session several times a day, and you see the cockatiel is showing calm behavior throughout the session and is moving to the perch faster, you can move to the next incremental step. After several successful repetitions of opening and closing the cage door slowly, one inch at a time, practice getting the cockatiel to station on the perch for 10 seconds.

 ## Putting It All Together: Goal Station Training

Before you start the training

1. The human needs to be in the mood to train. If you are not in a happy-go-lucky mood, do not train. Cockatiels can read our body language better than we can. If your cockatiel observes sluggish or "whatever" human body language, the bird may not train.
2. Make sure that the cockatiel has had several hours of not eating its favorite food item.
3. Have a couple of the favorite food items in your back pocket or in the palm of your hand so the cockatiel is focused on you and not the yummy item. We do not want to cue the cockatiel that you have the yummy items. (I would recommend four to six broken pieces of the yummy items so you can do several repetitions of the steps.)
4. Ensure the cockatiel is in the cage (and not all worked up) to start.

Putting it all together session:

1. The cockatiel should be in the cage.
2. You should be standing about one foot away from the cage.
3. Slowly approach the front of the cage, tap your finger once by the designated perch, cueing the stationing behavior.
    i. Do not show the yummy item (we want to fade out the lure).

4. When the cockatiel comes to the perch, wait until two feet are on the perch, then open the cage door.
    i. If the cockatiel stays on the perch
        - Say "Good," or PRAISE, PRAISE.
        - Either directly give the yummy item to the cockatiel or place the yummy item in the bowl by the perch.
        - Go to step 5.
    ii. If the cockatiel does not stay on the perch, close the cage door.
        - Go back to **Incremental Step 5: Stationing to the Perch (duration)** and work on more repetitions.
5. While the cockatiel is eating the food, close the cage door.

Don't rush it; every cockatiel learns differently. Go at your cockatiel's pace.

When your cockatiel starts coming out of the cage, you can tap the perch to have the cockatiel return to it. You can use all these steps to reteach stationing at another new location. Every new location is a new training situation for the cockatiel to relearn the behavior. Over time, the cockatiel will learn that stationing can happen anywhere.

Stepping Up Training

Stepping up training is an important skill because this teaches the cockatiel to come to you.

- During the initial session, the training is to have your cockatiel learn to step up on your hand, perch, or a ladder based on your cockatiel's comfort level.
- There are some cockatiels who are nervous about stepping up on a human hand because a hand or arm is not a solid surface like a tree branch.
- Stepping up training can lead to other training, such as recall and scale training.
- Teaching stepping up consists of several chained behaviors:

    Behavior 1: Desensitizing – Introducing a new object (follows the same beginning steps as target training)

    Behavior 2: Stationing – The cockatiel is starting at stationing to a location.

    And then there are two more additional steps:

    Behavior 3: Stepping up – The cockatiel is learning to step up on a new object.

Stepping up is not about pushing your finger against the chest of the cockatiel to force the cockatiel to step up. This training method may lead to the cockatiel learning to bite or avoiding working with you. The end goal is to allow the cockatiel to learn at its own pace, have fun, and have a respectful relationship with you.

The step-by-step training below starts with using a ladder, as this is going to become an extension of your hand. This process assists some cockatiels that already have a fear response to hands and assists those cockatiels that do not have a fear response with learning that the ladder is an extension of a hand. This approach comes in very handy when a cockatiel flies to a location we cannot reach with our hands, and we can use the wooden ladder to have the cockatiel step on.

Setting up the Environment

Supplies needed:

- A wooden ladder – the length of the ladder should fit through the cage door and be long enough to go about halfway into the cage while you hold it from the outside.
- Rope perch - If a wooden ladder cannot be found, a long rope perch can be used.
- Favorite food items

Before you start the training

1. The human needs to be in the mood to train. If you are not in a happy-go-lucky mood, do not train. Cockatiels can read our body language better than we can. If your cockatiel observes sluggish or "whatever" human body language, the bird may not train.
2. Make sure that the cockatiel has had several hours of not eating its favorite food item (like bite-sized walnuts).

Shaping toward Step Up – Part 1 – Introduction of the Ladder

This is the beginner step to start teaching the cockatiel that when the ladder appears, food will be delivered. The end goal is to be able to place and take out the ladder without triggering the cockatiel's fear response.

Incremental Step 01 ▶ Desensitization of the Ladder

1. The cockatiel should be in the cage.
2. You should be standing about three feet away from the front of the cage.
   - Start by holding the ladder behind your back in one hand. The yummy item should be in the other hand.
3. As you are standing three feet away from the front of the cage, slowly move the ladder from behind you to directly in front of you.
   - You do not have to say anything.
   - Do not wiggle the ladder. You really want it not to be a big deal for the bird.
4. Observe the cockatiel's body language before proceeding.

If the cockatiel is not screaming, squawking, pacing, flying, flopping to the bottom of the cage, or freaking out:

 PROCEED:

   i. Say "Good," and remember to PRAISE, PRAISE.
   ii. Move the ladder behind you or place it on the floor.
   iii. While the ladder is behind you or on the floor, walk slowly up to the cockatiel's cage and drop a piece of yummy food into the food bowl. Or, if you can (carefully) hand-feed the cockatiel, do so with your hand directly in front of the bird.
   iv. Go to Step 5

If the cockatiel is screaming, squawking, pacing, or the feathers are all fluffed up:

CHAPTER 10: Training Essentials

🛑 **DO NOT PROCEED:**

  i. Wait until the cockatiel's behavior settles down.
     - If the cockatiel's behavior settles down quickly, take a step back and go back to Step 3 (at the new distance) and try another attempt at the training.
     - If the cockatiel's behavior does not settle down quickly, end the session (no treat is given).
     - End the session.
  ii. During the next repetition, back up another foot or move the ladder slower, and that will be your new starting point.

5. Go back to Step 2 and do one repetition, and then take a break.

You can do this step several times a day. As long as the cockatiel shows calm behavior throughout several training repetitions, you can move to the next step.

Your next training steps proceed the same as the target training, moving closer to the cage each time without triggering the cockatiel's fear response.

Incremental Step 2 ▶ Desensitization of the Ladder (opening the cage door)

This is the next beginner step to start to teach the cockatiel that when the ladder appears in the cage, food will be delivered.

1. The cockatiel should be in the cage.
2. You should be standing in front of the cage with the ladder held next to you by your side.
3. Show the bird the ladder from outside the cage and slowly open the cage door just a few inches. Do not put the ladder through the cage door.
     - If your cockatiel still has fear responses with the cage door opening, then see if the ladder can fit through another cage opening.

- You can additionally try to do target training to direct the cockatiel to a perch far from the door before doing this session.
- You do not have to say anything.

4. Observe the cockatiel's body language before proceeding.

If the cockatiel is not screaming, squawking, pacing, flying, flopping to the bottom of the cage, or freaking out:

 PROCEED:

i. Say "Good," and remember to PRAISE, PRAISE.
ii. Close the door. (You have not put the ladder in the opening yet; you are just practicing opening the cage door enough so the ladder can fit.)
iii. Drop a piece of yummy food into the cockatiel's food bowl or directly give food to the cockatiel.
iv. Go to Step 5.

If the cockatiel is screaming, squawking, pacing, or its feathers are all fluffed up:

 DO NOT PROCEED:

i. Wait until the cockatiel's behavior settles down.
- If the cockatiel's behavior settles down quickly, take a step back and go back to Step 3, and try another attempt at the training.
- If the cockatiel's behavior does not settle down quickly, end the session (no treat is given).
- End the session.

5. Go back to Step 2 and do one repetition, and then take a break.

NOTE:

Try doing this session once or twice a day, if possible. If you can do this session several times a day, and you see the cockatiel is showing calm behavior throughout the session, then you can move to the next step.

CHAPTER 10: Training Essentials

Incremental Step 3 ▶ Desensitization of the Ladder (opening the cage door for the ladder)

1. The cockatiel should be in the cage.
2. You should be standing in front of the cage with the ladder held next to you by your side.
3. Slowly open the cage door just enough that the ladder can fit and place the far end of the ladder in the cage door opening.
   - If your cockatiel still has fear responses with the cage door opening, then see if the ladder can fit through another cage opening.
     - You can additionally try to do target training to direct the cockatiel to a perch far from the door before doing this session.
   - You do not have to say anything. Just the first rung of the ladder should go through the cage door.
4. Observe the cockatiel's body language before proceeding:

If the cockatiel is not screaming, squawking, pacing, flying, flopping to the bottom of the cage, or freaking out:

 PROCEED:

   i. Say "Good," and remember to PRAISE, PRAISE.
   ii. Remove the ladder and close the door.
   iii. Drop a piece of yummy food into the cockatiel's food bowl or directly give food to the cockatiel.
   iv. Go to Step 5.

If the cockatiel is screaming, squawking, pacing, or its feathers are all fluffed up:

 DO NOT PROCEED:

   i. Remove the ladder and close the cage door.
      - Wait until the cockatiel's behavior settles down.
      - If the cockatiel's behavior settles down quickly, go back to Step 3, and try another attempt at the training.

- If the cockatiel's behavior does not settle down quickly, end the session (no treat is given).
- End the session.

5. Go back to Step 2 and do one repetition, and then take a break.

NOTE:

Try doing this session once or twice a day, if possible. If you can do this session several times a day, and you see the cockatiel is showing calm behavior throughout the session, move to the next step.

Incremental Step 04 ▸ Moving the Ladder into the Cage.

1. The cockatiel should be in the cage.
2. You should be standing in front of the cage with the ladder held next to you by your side.
3. Show the bird the ladder from outside the cage and slowly open the cage.
4. Slowly open the cage door just enough that the ladder can fit, and move the far end of the ladder into the cage door opening, so only two rungs go into the cage.
5. Observe the cockatiel's body language before proceeding:

If the cockatiel is not screaming, squawking, pacing, flying, flopping to the bottom of the cage, or freaking out:

 PROCEED:

   i. Say "Good," and remember to PRAISE, PRAISE.
   ii. Close the door. Do not put the ladder in the opening yet; you are just practicing opening the cage door enough so the ladder can fit.
   iii. Drop a piece of yummy food into the cockatiel's food bowl or directly give the food to the cockatiel.

CHAPTER 10: Training Essentials

  iv. Go to Step 5.

If the cockatiel is screaming, squawking, pacing, or its feathers are all fluffed up:

 DO NOT PROCEED:

  i. Wait until the cockatiel's behavior settles down.
- If the cockatiel's behavior settles down quickly, take a step back and go back to Step 3 (at the new distance), and try another attempt at the training.
- If the cockatiel's behavior does not settle down quickly, end the session (no treat is given).
- End the session.

6. Go back to Step 2 and do one repetition, and then take a break.

NOTE:

Try doing this session once or twice a day, if possible. If you can do this session several times a day, and you see the cockatiel is showing calm behavior throughout the session, try to do these same steps, but move the ladder into the cage one rung at a time. Do not rush it, and if the cockatiel shows a fear response, back up to a step where the cockatiel appears calm.

Incremental Step 5 ▶ Ladder in the Cage

1. The cockatiel should be in the cage.
2. You should be standing in front of the cage with the ladder held next to you by your side.
3. Slowly open the cage door and place the ladder between the cage door opening to a perch inside the cage or to the back of the cage.
4. Observe the cockatiel's body language before proceeding.

If the cockatiel is not screaming, squawking, pacing, flying, flopping to the bottom of the cage, or freaking out:

 PROCEED:

    i. Say "Good," and remember to PRAISE, PRAISE.
    ii. Drop a piece of yummy food into the cockatiel's food bowl or directly give food to the cockatiel.
    iii. Slowly remove the ladder. You can leave the door open if the cockatiel will not fly out. If you are not sure, then close the cage door.
    iv. Go to Step 5.

If the cockatiel is screaming, squawking, pacing, or its feathers are all fluffed up:

 DO NOT PROCEED:

    i. Wait until the cockatiel's behavior settles down.
- If the cockatiel's behavior settles down quickly without removing the ladder, go to Step 4 for "Go-Proceed" where you will praise the positive behavior.
- If the cockatiel's behavior does not settle down quickly, end the session (no treat is given).
   - ✓ Remove the ladder and close the cage door.
   - ✓ End the session and go back to a previous step where the cockatiel was successful.

5. Go back to Step 3 and do one repetition, and then take a break.

NOTE:

Try doing this session once or twice a day, if possible. If you can do this session several times a day, and you see the cockatiel is showing calm behavior throughout the session, try to do these same steps, but move the ladder into the cage one rung at a time. Do not rush it, and if the cockatiel shows a fear response, back up to a step where the cockatiel appears calm.

CHAPTER 10: Training Essentials

Shaping toward Step Up – Part 2 – Introduction of the Stepping up Training

In the previous step, the cockatiel was learning that fun things happen on the ladder.

In this step, the cockatiel is going to continue learning that great things happen on the ladder. This session teaches the cockatiel that the ladder and hand have value and are safe places to receive yummy treats.

Before you start the training

- The human needs to be in the mood to train. If you are not in a happy-go-lucky mood, do not train. Cockatiels can read our body language better than we can. If your cockatiel observes sluggish or "whatever" human body language, the bird may not train.
- Make sure that the cockatiel has had several hours of not eating its favorite food item (like bite-sized walnuts).

Incremental Step 01 Luring with Food:

Once you can successfully put the ladder into the cage and place your hand on the ladder, the next step is luring the cockatiel to your hand.

1. The cage door is open, and the ladder is placed.
2. Place a hand flat on the ladder near the cage door.
3. Place a long millet branch on the ladder and hold the tip of the branch that is on the ladder (at the far end by the cage door).
4. Wait to see if the cockatiel goes to the branch (even if it's hanging on the cage to get to it).

If the cockatiel is not screaming, squawking, pacing, flying, flopping to the bottom of the cage, or freaking out:

 **PROCEED:**

   i. If the cockatiel comes over and starts eating the millet:
      - Say "Good," and remember to PRAISE, PRAISE.

- Let the cockatiel eat some of the millet, and when the cockatiel appears to be done eating, slowly move your hand and the millet out of the cage.
- Take a break, and try again a little later.

If the cockatiel is screaming, squawking, pacing, or its feathers are all fluffed up:

 DO NOT PROCEED:

   i. Remove the millet and your hand.
   ii. During the next repetition, place your hand on the ladder (at the end outside the cage door), and using that same hand, place the millet on the ladder. If the cockatiel prefers this setup, continue the training but keep your hand wrapped around the ladder rung.

5. Try one more repetition, and then end the session

Once the cockatiel is an expert at eating millet while you are holding the ladder, go to the next step.

Incremental Step 2 ▶ Luring with Food:

Once you can successfully put the ladder into the cage and place your hand on the ladder, the next step is luring the cockatiel to your hand.

1. The cage door is open, and the ladder is placed.
2. Place a hand flat on the ladder near the cage door.
3. Place a smaller millet branch on the ladder and hold the tip of the millet just barely on the ladder near the cage door.
4. Wait to see if the cockatiel comes over to you.

If the cockatiel is not screaming, squawking, pacing, flying, flopping to the bottom of the cage, or freaking out:

 PROCEED:

   i. If the cockatiel comes over and starts eating the millet
      - Say "Good," and remember to PRAISE, PRAISE.
      - Let the cockatiel eat some millet, and when the bird

CHAPTER 10: Training Essentials

appears to be done eating, slowly move the millet out of the cage.
- Take a break, and try again a little later.

If the cockatiel is screaming, squawking, pacing, or its feathers are all fluffed up:

 DO NOT PROCEED:

   i. Remove the millet and your hand.
   ii. Go back to Increment Step 1.

5. Try one more repetition, and then end the session

Once the cockatiel is an expert at eating millet while you are holding the ladder, go to the next step.

Incremental Step 3 ▸ Luring with Food:

Once you can successfully put the ladder into the cage and place your hand on the ladder, the next step is luring the cockatiel to your hand.

1. The cage door is open, and the ladder is placed.
2. Place a hand flat on the ladder near the cage door.
3. Place a smaller millet branch on the ladder and hold the tip of the millet on the far side of the ladder near the cage door.
4. Wait to see if the cockatiel comes over to you.

If the cockatiel is not screaming, squawking, pacing, flying, flopping to the bottom of the cage, or freaking out:

 PROCEED:

   i. If the cockatiel comes over and starts eating the millet
       - Say "Good," and remember to PRAISE, PRAISE.
       - Let the cockatiel eat some millet, and when the bird appears to be done eating, slowly move the millet out of the cage.
       - Take a break, and try again a little later.

If the cockatiel is screaming, squawking, pacing, or its feathers are all fluffed up:

 DO NOT PROCEED:

   i. Remove the millet and your hand.
      - Go back to Increment Step 2.

5. Try one more repetition, and then end the session

Once the cockatiel is an expert at eating millet while you are holding the ladder, go to the next step.

Incremental Step 04 Luring with Food:

Once you can successfully put the ladder into the cage and place your hand on the ladder, the next step is luring the cockatiel to your hand.

1. The cage door is open, and the ladder is placed.
2. Place a hand flat on the ladder near the cage door.
3. Place a smaller branch of millet (one- or two-inch length) between your finger and thumb, facing upright on the ladder near the cage door.
4. Wait to see if the cockatiel comes over to you.

If the cockatiel is not screaming, squawking, pacing, flying, flopping to the bottom of the cage, or freaking out:

 PROCEED:

   i. If the cockatiel comes over and starts eating the millet
      - Say "Good," and remember to PRAISE, PRAISE.
      - Let the cockatiel eat the millet.
      - Take a break, and try again a little later.

If the cockatiel is screaming, squawking, pacing, or its feathers are all fluffed up:

 DO NOT PROCEED:

   i. Remove the millet and your hand.

CHAPTER 10: Training Essentials

- Go back to Increment Step 3.

5. Try one more repetition, and then end the session.

Once the cockatiel is an expert at eating millet while you are holding the ladder, go to the next step.

Incremental Step 5  Luring with food:

Once you can successfully put the ladder into the cage and place your hand on the ladder, the next step is luring the cockatiel to your hand.

1. The cage door is open, and the ladder is placed.
2. Place a hand flat on the ladder near the cage door.
3. Place a smaller branch of millet (one- or two-inch length) between your finger and thumb, facing upright on the ladder by the cage door.
4. Wait to see if the cockatiel comes over to you.

If the cockatiel is not screaming, squawking, pacing, flying, flopping to the bottom of the cage, or freaking out:

GO PROCEED:

   i. If the cockatiel comes over and starts eating the millet
      - Wait and see if the cockatiel starts to put one foot on your hand (or touches your hand).
      - Say, "Good."
      - Let the cockatiel eat the millet.
      - Take a break and try again a little later.

If the cockatiel is screaming, squawking, pacing, or its feathers are all fluffed up:

 DO NOT PROCEED:

   i. Remove the millet and your hand.
      - Go back to Increment Step 4.

5. Try one more repetition, and then end the session.

- What if the cockatiel stays on your hand? You can wait until the cockatiel eats all the millet or let go of the millet so it falls off your hand.

Once the cockatiel is an expert at eating millet while you're holding the ladder, go to the next step.

Incremental Step 6 ▶ Stepping Up (Moving the Food):

Once you can successfully put the ladder into the cage and place your hand on the ladder, the next step is luring the cockatiel to your hand.

1. The cage door is open, and the ladder is placed.
2. Place a hand flat on the ladder near the cage door.
3. Place a smaller branch of millet (one- or two-inch length) between the finger and thumb of the opposite hand. Your other hand should be flat on the ladder.
4. Wait to see if the cockatiel comes over to you.

If the cockatiel is not screaming, squawking, pacing, flying, flopping to the bottom of the cage, or freaking out:

 PROCEED:

   i. If the cockatiel comes over and starts to step up on your hand and eat the millet:
      - Say, "Step up."
      - Let the cockatiel eat the millet.
      - Do not move your hand.
      - Let the cockatiel leave the hand when done.

If the cockatiel is screaming, squawking, pacing, or its feathers are all fluffed up:

 DO NOT PROCEED:

   i. Remove the millet and your hand.
   ii. Go back to **Incremental Step 4**.

5. Try one more repetition, and then end the session.

- What if the cockatiel does not leave your hand? Just let go of the millet and let the cockatiel step off when the cockatiel is ready.

 Putting It All Together: Stepping Up Training

Before you start the training

1. The human needs to be in the mood to train. If you are not in a happy-go-lucky mood, do not train. Cockatiels can read our body language better than we can. If your cockatiel observes sluggish or "whatever" human body language, the bird may not train.
2. Make sure that the cockatiel has had several hours of not eating its favorite food item.
3. Have a couple of the bird's favorite food items in your back pocket or in the palm of your hand so the cockatiel is focused on you and not the yummy item. We do not want to cue the cockatiel that you have the yummy items. (I would recommend four to six broken pieces of the yummy items so you can do several repetitions of the steps.)
4. Ensure the cockatiel is in the cage (and not all worked up) to start.

Putting it all together session:

1. The cage door is open, and the ladder is placed.
2. Place a hand flat on the ladder near the cage door.
3. Say "Step Up."
4. Wait to see if the cockatiel comes over to you.
   i. If the cockatiel comes over and two feet step up on the hand
      - Say, "Good."
      - Give the bird millet from your other hand.
      - Do not move your hand. Let the cockatiel leave the hand when the bird is done.

ii. If the cockatiel does not come over, place millet on your hand and go back to Step 4.
- If the cockatiel still does not come over, go back to Step 4.

When the cockatiel starts stepping up more and more on your hand, wait a second and then move your hand up one inch. If the cockatiel stays on the hand:

- Say, "Good."
- Give the bird millet from your other hand.
- Move your hand back to the starting position so the cockatiel can choose to step off.
- If the cockatiel does not want to step off, you can use millet to lure it off your hand.

Conclusion

Training is very important. The most important part of training is to understand how to create small successful steps to reach the main goal. Your cockatiel does not know how to do something immediately. There need to be incremental steps that become consistent, repetitive training. Do not rush the cockatiel through the steps; take your time, have patience, and success will happen.

When learning the steps of Target Training, Station Training, and Step Up Training, these processes can be intertwined to step up off the station perch to target training and back to the station perch.

These are just the beginning training lessons, which can lead to further advanced training.

CHAPTER 10: Training Essentials

Additional Resources

If you are looking for additional resources on training or understanding behavior:

1. Barbara Heidenreich – Force Free Animal Training (https://barbarasffat.com/)
2. Lara Joseph – The Animal Behavior Center (https://www.theanimalbehaviorcenter.com/)
3. International Associate of Animal Behavior Consultants (https://iaabc.org/)

CHAPTER 11

Breeding

Be Responsible

Throughout this book, we've looked at the responsibility and amount of dedicated work it takes to care for a single cockatiel. That responsibility and workload grow exponentially the more birds you have. But if you're

Photo Courtesy of Jeannie Terry

completely smitten and feel your calling is to breed cockatiels, this chapter will give you a big-picture view of what it takes to become a breeder.

Many of the guidelines concerning health, diet, and behavior you learned in previous chapters are equally important, if not more so, when running a hatchery. Plus, there are some things you need to ask yourself before proceeding. Do you have homes for the babies? Because you'll need buyers and an outlet through which to sell baby cockatiels. There's the business side of running a hatchery, reporting earnings, etc. Finally, there are hours upon hours of cleaning, feeding, and attending to multiple birds. So weigh your decision in this as carefully as you did your initial cockatiel purchase.

Unfertilized

I shared how my family had our cockatiel Sheldon for months before he laid an egg, and we discovered he was a female and became Shelly. This is quite common in cockatiels. Females can lay unfertilized eggs without ever having been around a male. Don't be alarmed if you see your cockatiel throw an egg out of the nest. If she decides to sit on it, allow her to. Females will normally abandon unfertilized eggs after three weeks or so. You can remove them one at a time, once every few days. This will help the cockatiel understand they are unfertile.

Bonded Pair

One of the first things to consider is the birds you want to breed. The issue with this is you can't force cockatiels to mate. Simply putting them together in a cage doesn't guarantee they will bond, and they will only breed if they are bonded. Unfortunately, even if two birds bond, that doesn't necessarily mean they are the opposite sex and can mate. Remember, cockatiels are very affectionate and sometimes bond with the same sex or even you, being exclusive in sharing their attention.

Male cockatiels need to be at least 18 months old, and female cockatiels need to be two years old to breed. It's around these times that the birds are emotionally mature enough to breed. If the female is too young, she may not sit on the eggs. So, as with buying your first cockatiel, you'll need to know who you're buying your breeding birds from to be certain of their ages and genders.

Mating Conditions

Besides an acceptable mate, there are other conditions that facilitate mating. Adequate nutrition is at the top of the list. The hen requires a balanced diet for fertility. She'll need cuttlebone for calcium and a good source of protein, plus the nutrients derived from fresh vegetables. Increased daylight in the room will help. Cockatiels in the wild are seasonal breeders, and daylight will mimic summer days. Their mating season is the rainy season, so temperature and humidity levels will also affect their mating.

Mating

Cockatiels are monogamous birds. They will remain with the same mate throughout each breeding season. When it's time to mate, the male cockatiel will sing a song and perform a dance for the female. He'll bob his head and hop around to attract her attention. They'll also groom and preen each other. And when the female is ready to mate, she'll show it by crouching down. It's normal for the pair to mate more than once when the female gets ready to lay eggs, and they will mate even after she starts to lay. They don't always mate in the same place, so allow them to choose where they want. Once they've mated, the female will lay her eggs within one to two weeks. Like many other types of birds, a female may lay one egg every other day until they have all been laid, so it can take one or two weeks to lay the whole clutch. When it comes to sitting on the eggs, the male and female share the task, taking shifts. The father is as attentive as the mother and will watch over his little family.

CHAPTER 11: Breeding

Nesting Box

In the wild, cockatiels nest in holes in trees or branches, and they don't usually use any nesting material. Domestic cockatiels use a nest called a breeding box. It's best to provide them with some kind of nesting material when using a breeding box. This keeps the eggs from moving around and ensures the box is dry. If the female doesn't have a nest box, she may lay her eggs on the cage floor, which can cause them to be crushed or stepped on.

Nesting boxes can be bought, but you can also make your own out of cardboard boxes. As for the nesting materials, shredded paper, paper lining, or molted feathers work well. Nest boxes can cramp your cockatiels' living space, so, if possible, try to attach the box outside of the cage. This will maintain the bird's living space and allow you to see what's going on inside the nest box.

Eggs

You may wonder how to tell if your female cockatiel is pregnant. Here are a few signs to watch for.

- Consuming more calcium: Pregnant females will eat more cuttlebone than usual to build up their calcium.
- Drinking more water: The water is necessary for the developing eggs, and the bird may want to bathe more often.
- Weight gain: You may notice your bird gaining a few ounces.
- Feathers: The bird's feathers may be puffier than usual.
- Nest: She may be spending more time around the nest.
- Larger droppings: Because eggs take up space in a cockatiel's torso, it won't have bowel movements as often, so the droppings will be larger and more odorous.
- Swollen abdomen: When pregnant, the cockatiel will appear fuller around the abdomen and vent.
- Nest preparation: The female may shred paper and bedding for the nest.

Cockatiels will lay one to two clutches of eggs a year. Birds in captivity will lay once every six months, and each clutch will have two to eight eggs. In Chapter 8, we touched on egg binding. Egg binding is considered an emergency medical condition with the potential to cause death. If you plan on breeding, you need to stay mindful of the signs. If you see any of these signs in your cockatiel, go to the vet immediately.

Signs of Egg Binding

- Labored breathing
- Puffed-up feathers

CHAPTER 11: Breeding

- Swelling
- Straining
- Loss of appetite
- Sitting on the cage floor for extended periods of time
- Constipation
- Tail bobbing
- Vomiting
- Paralysis of one or both legs

Incubation

On average, cockatiels incubate their eggs for about 18 to 20 days. This can vary by a couple of days in either direction, but it's no cause for concern. Don't touch or remove the eggs unless they are cracked or broken, which can lead to the spread of bacteria.

Egg turning is the act of turning an egg over during incubation to prevent the embryo from sticking to the shell and dying. Aviculturists frequently inspect nest boxes and candle eggs to check for fertility.

However, newly paired or less tame pairs can be more stressed when they are disturbed. It's best to leave them alone so they don't accidentally damage the unhatched eggs.

Most experts suggest you turn the eggs for them to remain viable. Otherwise, the eggs may not hatch. Egg turning also allows the embryo to encounter fresh nutrients inside the egg. If possible, eggs should be turned every hour. If not, at least a minimum of five times a day. This must be done every day until day 16 of the incubation. The eggs are not to be turned in the final three days. Be sure to take precautions and wash your hands thoroughly before handling the eggs, and be gentle. Your cockatiel should be amenable to your care of the eggs, as they don't usually object to people handling them.

Hatching and Beyond

Hatching can take a few hours or a couple of days. Chicks will hatch every other day just as they were laid. The chick inside will use an egg tooth to chip its way out. The crack it makes is called a pip, and the process is called pipping. It may be tempting, but don't assist the bird in

Photo Courtesy of Eve Cusac-Seale

pipping. There are mixed opinions about assisting chicks in the hatching process, but you could easily harm one of the delicate babies.

After the chicks are born, you may find them resting on their backs in the nest. Hatching is hard work. For the next eight to 12 hours, the parents will keep the little ones warm. They won't feed them right away, as the chicks will receive nourishment from absorbing the yolk sac. Baby cockatiels stay with their parents for 10 to 12 weeks, and as with the nesting process, both parents continue to take care of the clutch after the hatching.

There are times an egg won't hatch. This could be because your cockatiel is still too young. She may lack the nutrients to produce a viable egg. The egg may not be fertilized, or the chick inside could be dead.

If you plan to allow the cockatiels to raise the chicks, be sure to keep their food supply filled. The male and female continue to need extra nutrition during this time for themselves and the feeding of the babies.

One Final Thing to Consider

We've established cockatiels are affectionate birds. They love, and they love deeply. So, if you have children in the home, bear in mind the emotional connection they will make with your birds. It can be hard when an egg is broken or a chick dies, not to mention your heart and its connection to the cockatiels. Be prepared and be responsible.

Glossary

Antecedent - An event/action that occurs before initiating a behavior; this can include cues, luring, and previously learned events.

Antecedent Arrangement – Setting up the environment to improve the probability that the companion cockatiel will do the behavior or take a step closer to the goal behavior.

Behavior – Any observed action a companion cockatiel does in a specific environment.

Captured Behavior – Reinforcing the cockatiel to achieve a specific behavior without cues or prompts. The cockatiel just does the specific behavior.

Consequence – An event/action that occurs immediately following a behavior that increases the likelihood of the behavior happening again.

Counter Conditioning – The cockatiel's conditioned emotional response to a stimulus is replaced with an opposite response.

Counter Conditioning Systematic Desensitization – The cockatiel's conditioned emotional response to a stimulus is gradually exposed to gain a neutral or opposite response.

Cue – Antecedent event/action that indicates the start of a specific designated behavior.

Luring – Improves the likelihood of getting a target behavior by showing the companion cockatiel the reinforcer before the behavior. (Luring should be faded out when the companion cockatiel begins learning the behavior).

Reinforcer – A consequence that increases the probability of a specific behavior. The companion cockatiel selects the reinforcer.

Reinforcement – The process by which a consequence increases (strengthens) or maintains the behavior.

Shaping – The process of reinforcing successful small steps to create the final desired behavior.

Stimulus – A change in the environment that causes a behavior.

References

1. **American Veterinary Society of Animal Behavior**
   Position Statement on Humane Dog Training
   (2021)
   https://avsab.org/wp-content/uploads/2021/08/AVSAB-Humane-Dog-Training-Position-Statement-2021.pdf?fbclid=IwAR03Om-iyhLYhoz-3tMHGhSY u_72gn98ZksR025rM-wGcWsBesbcoH9Jmmk

2. **S.G. Friedman Ph.D.**
   "How Parrots Learn to Behave"
   Cockatiel Talk,
   (May 2003)
   https://www.behaviorworks.org/files/articles/How%20Parrots%20Learn%20Behavior%202003.pdf

3. **S.G. Friedman Ph.D.**
   "Pavlov's Parrots: Understanding and Extinguishing Fear Triggers"
   Good Cockatiel Magazine
   (June 2007)
   https://www.behaviorworks.org/files/articles/Pavlov's%20Parrots.pdf

4. **Hillary Hankey**
   "What's the Difference in Using Systematic Desensitization versus Counter Conditioning in Animal Training?"
   Avian Behavior International
   (Aug 2019)
   https://avian-behavior.org/systematic-desensitization-counter-conditioning/

5. **SeaWorld Parks & Entertainment**
   "Animal Behavior & Training – Definition of Behavior"
   SeaWorld Parks & Entertainment
   (2023)
   https://seaworld.org/animals/all-about/training/animal-behavior-and-learning/

www.ingramcontent.com/pod-product-compliance
Lightning Source LLC
LaVergne TN
LVHW020133080526
838202LV00047B/3931